Just
DON'T
QUIT!

DESTINY IMAGE BOOKS BY JOAN HUNTER

The Power of Prophetic Vision

Healing Starts Now!
Expanded Edition: Complete Training Manual

Just
DON'T
QUIT!

INSPIRATION TO FULFILL
YOUR GOD-SIZED DREAMS

Joan Hunter

DESTINY IMAGE® PUBLISHERS, INC.

P.O. Box 310, Shippensburg, PA 17257-0310

"Promoting Inspired Lives."

This book and all other Destiny Image and Destiny Image Fiction books are available at Christian bookstores and distributors worldwide.

Cover design by Eileen Rockwell

Interior design by Terry Clifton

For more information on foreign distributors, call 717-532-3040.

Reach us on the Internet: www.destinyimage.com.

ISBN 13 TP: 978-0-7684-5746-9

ISBN 13 eBook: 978-0-7684-5747-6

ISBN 13 HC: 978-0-7684-5640-0

ISBN 13 LP: 978-0-7684-5639-4

For Worldwide Distribution, Printed in the U.S.A.

1 2 3 4 5 6 7 8 / 25 24 23 22 21

CONTENTS

Chapter One

JUST DON'T QUIT!

I'm so excited about this book because, through the years in ministry, I personally have had many opportunities to quit. But I didn't. I chose to stay on the path God had called me to. Sometimes we fall in a ditch; sometimes we get *pushed* into the ditch. What do we do when that happens? A better question would be, "What should we do?"

Through life's battles and experiences, many people have thought about quitting, and some have given up. Even if you have quit, this is the time to get back up and do what you were created to do. God has certainly not given up on you.

In this book, you will find many answers to your questions about getting up and moving to the sound of God's voice and according to His Word. You will also discover many testimonies of people who thought about quitting, had laid their dreams down, and now they are actually living their dreams. They pushed through the tough times, persevered, and overcame.

I want you to live your dream, do what you were born to do, and discover the happiest life ever!

One of my favorite sayings by Winston Churchill is "Never give up!" I have that theme throughout my house. Go over, go under, go through, go around, but *never* give up!

The battle for my life actually started when I was still nestled in my mother's womb. Her pregnancy popped up at a very inopportune time in her life. Her relationship with my father was not positive. In fact, during her pregnancy, my father arrived with a pistol in his hand and tried to kill Mom, which would have also ended my life.

During my school years, I endured name calling and negative branding from kids and teachers alike. The most prominent title was even spouted by my brother: "Dumb, Dumb."

Many years passed before my learning disabilities and challenges were identified. Encouragement to improve or excel was absent.

One of the most important events of my life was Mom marrying Charles Hunter, who formally adopted me as a teenager. He very pointedly told me to stop referring to myself as "Dumb, Dumb!" I was to change my nickname to "Smart, Smart!"

When I got married, I had visions of a happy family serving God forever. Little did I realize that after the birth of four beautiful daughters and co-pastoring a great church for over eighteen years, I would receive the shock of my life. My husband was living a double life in an alternate lifestyle.

Divorce followed along with the dissolution of our church and loss of many dear friends. I had never had a secular job but had to seek employment to survive. I not only found a great job, I thrived being independent.

Instead of hiding behind the success of my internationally known parents and a talented and respected spouse, I had to find and develop my own confidence. I had to collapse into the arms of my Lord Jesus Christ and discover His will for my life.

Personally, I would not be here today if I had chosen to give up. I've gone through breast cancer, emotional ruin, financial ruin, to everything being literally stripped away from my family and me. Yet because I chose to hang on to God's promises, God has totally and completely restored everything in my life!

He directed me into the ministry I envisioned so many years ago. He has given me the strength to share my testimony over and over again to encourage others to walk with Him and depend on His promises.

Does my ministry just continue what my parents built? No, it has expanded the healing ministry that Charles and Frances began so many years ago. God has blessed me with so many more revelations to edify the Body of Christ.

Yes, JHM continues to pray for physical healing of the sick, but we now pray for total healing of body, mind, spirit, and finances.

Being open to God's will and leading, I can now share with and minister to people around the earth. Books, tapes, CDs, DVDs, TV shows, and, thanks to COVID, Zoom meetings over the internet allow widespread messages of His power and love to His children.

Testimonies of God's miracles are always fun to hear about. I have specifically asked special friends to compile their stories for this book. They have freely and lovingly opened their hearts to encourage you to believe God for your miracle also.

I believe that God will use this book to reveal to you what He has for you to do. Your hope will soar as you read the testimonies of those who decided not to give up. God is not a respecter of persons. What He has done for them, He can also do for you.

Allow Him to speak to your heart and reveal areas of your life where you gave up or began to give up on your dreams or visions. Repent for your part and give those areas back to God and watch what He will do. You were created on purpose, for a purpose, and with a purpose that you were predestined to fulfill. You can do this! He is still in the business of blessing His people with miracles!

"Miracles Happen!"

Joan Hunter

Chapter Two

RECOGNIZE YOUR FULL POTENTIAL

What would you do if you knew you could not fail?

God has a destiny planned for every child He has created. Before you give up on your destiny, let's look at a few people in the scriptures as well as faithful ones in today's world. God called each of them to fulfill a specific purpose. They could have run the other direction, and a few actually did.

However, in the end, they obeyed God's calling and made a tremendous contribution to the world. Can you imagine a Bible without these stories, which show us God's faithfulness, His children's hope and courage, and God's encouragement to all His children?

Moses

When God called him to return to Egypt and lead His people out of slavery, Moses had all kinds of excuses. He begged God to choose someone else. He said, "God, I cannot speak well. I stutter." Aaron stepped in to solve that issue. The Israelites followed Moses out of Egypt, across the Red Sea on dry land, and into the promised land of milk and honey. (Read Exodus, Leviticus, Numbers, and Deuteronomy.)

Two Loaves and Five Fish

This young boy felt like he only had a little to offer, but he was willing to give everything. "This is all I have." Jesus took that small amount of food and blessed it. That small offering multiplied to meet the needs of thousands of hungry people. (Read the story in Matthew 14 and Mark 6.)

Cheryl Prewitt Salem

In Cheryl's teenage years, the family was in a catastrophic automobile accident. She was thrown through the windshield, broke her back, and crushed her left leg. Her face required more than 100 stitches, and the doctors told her parents that there was a good chance she would never walk again. She was in a body cast from her chest to her toes on one side and from her chest to her knees on the other for four months. When the cast came off, her left leg was weak, lifeless and two full inches shorter than her right.

That car crash resulting in a physical handicap and over 100 stitches in her face were no match for what God had planned for her life. During a Kenneth Hagin meeting, Cheryl was healed.

Cheryl was called to be Miss America. She lost in five separate competitions before she was finally crowned Miss America in 1980. She and her family now serve God with the same kind of tenacity and commitment. Despite the death of their precious daughter and a personal battle with cancer, Cheryl is recognized as an American Christian evangelist, author, speaker, musician, and former beauty pageant titleholder as well as a wife and mother.

Oral Roberts

In his younger years, Oral stuttered and suffered with tuberculosis. He begged God to choose someone else to spread His message. During his years of preaching and teaching, Dr. Roberts received more negative press than any other human being at that time.

However, God used him to spread the ministry of healing through huge crusades across the country as well as radio and TV. In addition, Oral Roberts University has graduated countless thousands of Christian leaders who have spread His Word around the world.

Helen Keller

Helen became deaf and blind shortly after her birth due to a severe illness. She had a long battle ahead of her before she realized her potential. Did she recognize her full potential? If you asked her, she would reply, "NO!" What do you think?

She graduated from college with high honors. She went on to teach at the university level. Despite her disabilities, she gave what she had and asked God to make up the difference.

Billy Graham

This powerful preacher traveled across the US and around the world to share God's Word to hundreds of thousands of people. His radio and TV shows have been viewed and heard by millions through the years. Indeed, they still continue to be broadcast and reach the masses today.

His children now continue Billy's legacy. Billy was first called to serve God at age 16. He fought the good fight until his death at 99.

Abraham Lincoln

This man was called to be the President of the United States. Even though he was born of very modest means in a log cabin, he saw and took advantage of many opportunities that helped him to succeed.

He faced many instances of failure, but he didn't quit! For instance, he was a self-taught lawyer. He got hold of books and devoured the knowledge contained on those printed pages. He was a champion and he never gave up. He was a fighter. Did you know Lincoln is actually honored in the Wrestling Hall of Fame?

Looking at his many accomplishments, you must agree he was a fascinating character. He was an honest, hard-working man who survived more than his share of hardships and setbacks. He never gave up fighting for what was right.

He was elected President of the United States in 1860 and won a second term in 1864. Lincoln's Emancipation Proclamation issued on January 1, 1863 declared freedom for all slaves and gave blacks the right to serve in both the Army and the Navy of the Union. This is considered Lincoln's greatest accomplishment.

Lincoln's Gettysburg Address is well known in American history. He gave this speech at the dedication of the Soldiers' National Cemetery in Gettysburg, Pennsylvania on November 19, 1863. It is one of the most quoted presidential speeches ever given. He is often described as being extremely wise and moral.

Research his fascinating story. He had many opportunities to throw in the towel and give up. But Abraham Lincoln never gave up!

The Hero: Audie Murphy

Audie Murphy was born in Kingston, Texas, the son of a sharecropper. His father abandoned their family and his mother died when he was a teenager. Murphy dropped out of school in the fifth grade in order to work to help support his family.

After America declared war on Japan and Germany, Audie wanted to enter the military. His enlistment application was initially turned down by the Army, Navy, and the Marine Corps because he was too short, underage, and underweight. Eventually, Murphy was accepted in the Army.

During World War II, he fought in many battles across Europe. Murphy's feats of bravery during these battles were so numerous and spectacular that he became the most decorated American combat soldier in World War II. He received every decoration for valor the US military awarded at that time, including the Medal of Honor and five more awards from the French and Belgian governments.

After World War II, Audie Murphy carried on a two decade long acting career appearing in over 40 movies and numerous TV shows. Murphy has the unusual distinction of playing himself in the movie version of his own autobiography, *To Hell and Back*.

Murphy died in a plane crash in 1971. He was buried in Arlington Memorial Cemetery.

Murphy was awarded the Texas Legislative Medal of Honor after his death.

Obviously, Audie Murphy didn't allow anything to stop him. He never quit!

Colonel Sanders: A Name We All Know

Colonel Sanders had a rough life. He attempted many jobs and fought for success. He failed so many times. Like so many people, he retired at age sixty-five. Not long after that, he considered committing suicide.

He sat down to write his will, but instead, he wrote what he could have accomplished with his life. He realized there was much more that he hadn't yet done. There was one thing he could do better than anyone else he knew. He could cook.

He borrowed some money and bought some food. He prepared the food using his own recipe and went door to door to sell his creations.

By the age of eighty-eight, Colonel Sanders, founder of the Kentucky Fried Chicken (KFC) Empire, was a millionaire.

Colonel Sanders was a Spirit-filled man and very active in his church. He used his God-given talents to feed the people of God as well as the world. He faithfully gave over and above his regular tithes and offerings to several ministries.

Moral of the story: It is *never* too late to start all over.

Most importantly, it's all about your attitude. Never give up, no matter how hard things get.

You have what it takes to be successful. God's blessings are endless.

Go for it and make a difference.

Job

The book of Job in the Old Testament of the Bible chronicles his experiences with loss and turmoil. In just one day, Job lost everything except his wife and his life. All his children and possessions were destroyed. His wife and friends even turned against him. However, in spite of everything, Job stood strong. He never gave up! God blessed him many times over during the next portion of his life. (Read the book of Job.)

More stories to research in the Bible: Gideon, Noah, Daniel, Joseph, Jonah, Abraham, Paul, and Ruth. There are many more to discover as you search God's Word. Start with King David.

King David

David, the eighth and youngest son of Jesse, was small in stature as a teenager. He was a shepherd in his father's fields and played with rocks and his slingshot. When the sheep were in danger, he was skilled enough to chase off the wild animals with a rock and his simple hand-made slingshot. He was physically strong also. He killed a lion and a bear with his bare hands. David honored God and often sat in the countryside playing his lyre and worshiping with song.

There are many situations in our lives that appear to be overwhelming. There is always the potential for us to quit trying. David could never have succeeded in his God ordained purpose if he would have been overwhelmed by fear. In his father's fields, he protected the sheep and fought off the wild animals like a good shepherd should.

In some ways, he was an outcast. He spent most of his time with the animals. When Samuel came to Jesse's house looking for the next king to anoint, Jesse didn't even consider calling David from the field. Obviously, he was an afterthought and not esteemed as anything important or worthwhile in his father's eyes.

David was chosen by God and anointed by Samuel to be the next king. Everyone knew Saul was healthy and strong. How could the teenager, David, be the next king? I am sure David's family just shrugged their shoulders and went about their business while David returned to the fields.

Time passed and King Saul was in need of someone who was skilled at playing the lyre. David was summoned and employed at the palace to soothe Saul's mind with beautiful music.

Goliath came on the scene and held the entire area in fear. David went to feed his brothers and heard Goliath cursing Israel and God. David confronted the ten-foot-tall giant who wielded his weapons of war. David was triumphant with his simple slingshot and stones because he had God on his side.

David was promoted to a high rank in Saul's army and became a very successful warrior and leader. He was so successful, Saul became very jealous. While playing the lyre one day, David was nearly killed. In a fury of temper, Saul threw his spear and barely missed David. This happened twice. Barely escaping the unwarranted attack, David took to the hills.

Even though David was married to Saul's daughter and best friends with his son, Jonathan, Saul was determined to destroy David and continued to chase him around the countryside for several years. David had a death sentence hanging over his head while he hid from Saul and Saul's men.

Despite all the negative things whirling around David, he maintained his faith in God and hung on to His promises. David remembered Samuel anointing him to be the next king; however, that didn't seem possible. His story is exciting and inspiring. He never quit. He kept on going toward his destiny.

Read David's story in 1 Samuel and 2 Samuel. Could you endure all the issues David faced? Would you? With the Lord's help, David was victorious and became a "man after God's own heart." He also wrote many of the Psalms that we love today. They truly tell his story—the blessings and the challenges.

With God's direction and guidance, you can win your battles also! Sing His praises like David did! Stay in His presence! You, like David, have been anointed to serve God. Choose to follow Him and win!

History records many Christian martyrs who willingly gave up their lives instead of turning their backs on their Savior and Lord. Many of Jesus' own disciples fall into this category.

What Has God Said About You?

Have you received a prophetic word from God? Have you accepted what He has planned for you? Have you reached His goal for your life or have you stalled along your way?

We all have setbacks or roadblocks along our journey. It's up to each of us to decide what to do with them! People are often looking for an excuse to fail. When they find an excuse they like, they use it over and over again. Some common ones I hear include: my childhood was bad, my family came from difficult situations, I am too old (or too young), I was abused (child, spouse, women, and/or men), I am too poor (or too rich), not enough education, I am sick, I have a disability—the list goes on.

What did I have to offer God? Mom and Dad had all the talent. My spouse back then was accomplished in everything he did while I was hiding behind the curtain most of the time.

Every Christian needs to learn how to fight. I wasn't a fighter, but I had to learn. God wants your availability as well as your ability. He will make up the difference and teach you what to do.

Each of us has decisions to make. We have to choose to go with God or quit. There are opportunities to quit every day, every hour.

What did God say to you today?

How do we recognize our full potential? Start with:

- Seek His face continually (see 1 Chron. 16:11).
- Continue in My Word and you will know the truth and it will set you free (see John 8:31-32).

What would you do if you knew you could not fail?

Why aren't you doing it?

Make a list. Include the date you wrote the list and the date you completed each item. Don't write the list with "due dates" that are unrealistic.

I pray that you aren't wasting your life with excuses or unrealistic goals. Don't be convinced that you are worthless or have nothing to offer. Who's telling you those lies?

The enemy wants to stop you from reaching your destiny. If he can get you to ignore God, you won't be giving God your best. Your loaves and fishes will be wasted.

God is the God of the third, fourth, fifth, sixth chance. He is waiting for you. He wants to touch through me as well as through you. If you feel like you have let God down, let your church down, or let yourself down, pray with me right now. Come to the altar and let this be your prayer.

Father, forgive me for not listening to You and Your Holy Spirit. Open my eyes and ears so I can hear Your voice and walk into my destiny. Your Word says that I am Your child so I am a valuable part of Your chosen family. I willingly lay down what I have to offer to You, and I know You will multiply it to be used by the Body of Christ, which does include me. Touch through me. Work through me. Praise You, Father, for Your forgiveness, Your grace, and Your love. In Jesus' name. Amen.

Chapter Three

PAINT YOUR PICTURE

I am 53 years old and a missionary in Haiti. It has not always been a gospel way with me.

When I was young, I was raised by my father who was a minister.

At twelve years of age, I was smoking marijuana and popping pills. Little did I know that at fifteen, I would stick a needle in my arm. For about the next ten years, my life went down the wrong path. I was in multiple rehab facilities. Finally, when I was twenty-five, I moved to Houston, Texas. I continued drinking alcohol. Alcohol is a drug. I kept drinking and drinking and drinking. Soon, I was back on the drugs again.

God has always had His hand over my life. Even when I was in Houston, I had a great job at a Fortune 500 company and made very good money. I was a functional addict for many years. Fast forwarding to 35 years of age, I got very sick one night. They found I had Hepatitis C. I couldn't work because of the treatment I was on. I continued to do drugs and sell drugs.

Unfortunately, or fortunately for me, I got pulled over by the police one night. I had forgotten to fasten my seatbelt. I ended up with a bench warrant for not wearing a seatbelt. I have told people for years that a seatbelt saved my life.

I had sold some drugs to a friend. When he got busted for drugs, he told the police where he had gotten them. The police busted into the motel where I was living. I had already lost my home. They took me to jail with just my pants on. I lost everything—no wallet, no ID, no clothes. When

I got out, I found others had come into my room and pilfered everything.

But God had a plan since I was very young. My father was a tent evangelist and traveled up and down the east coast of the United States. I played the drums and sang with my mom and dad. People always said how blessed they were to hear us.

God had had His hand on me throughout all those rehab visits and even in South Africa. My father sent me on a missions trip, and I got in trouble there also.

It all caught up with me. Life like that will always catch up with you. God will catch you or you will die.

Life took a toll on me while I ran from God. You will always have two choices—run to God or run from Him. Now, I always say, "If you run from God long enough, you will run *into* Him."

I had to get a public defender to represent me so I could continue my liver treatments while I was in jail. I had pushed my limits. I was facing ten years hard time in prison.

The man who would testify against me left town so he would not have to appear in court. Without a witness, I was able to plead out. Instead of ten years, I got sentenced to two years in jail.

I was put in the area of jail with all the sick and ill inmates. That area was full of spirits of everything—infirmity, addiction, etc. I have always had a sense of spirituality and could actually see the darkness around me. In spite of everything, I remained in total denial of my condition. I would not admit to anyone that I was a drug addict.

While I was incarcerated, I was washing other inmates' clothes so I could get hold of their psych meds. It is crazy how that spirit of addiction had its claws in me. I actually overdosed on psych meds while I was in jail. You usually wash your own things, but I was "helping" others just to get their meds. Snorting meds, taking pills—I did everything I could get my hands on. I was doing anything I could do to get meds.

That was as close to being a prodigal as one can get. I was a prodigal and it caught up with me. I remember the gurney coming to pick me up to take me to the jail infirmary.

God sent a nurse to speak directly into my spirit about my issues and problems. When they rolled me in to pump my stomach, the nurse leaned over me and said, "Why did you do such a thing?"

I replied, "I am a drug addict and I need help."

The Holy Spirit started working in my life from that very moment. I had been in such denial about my situation. But the moment I acknowledged I had a problem, God had permission to reach down and help me. It was a complete turnaround in my life. The Holy Spirit started working on me.

They pumped my stomach and kept me overnight. Then I was sent back to that cell packed with sick, smelly men.

I told God, "Father, I know what I am now. I know You can help me, but I don't know what to do. I can't feel anything." My heart felt like stone.

God's Word tells us He will take our heart of stone and replace it with a heart of flesh. He did just that.

I found a Bible in my cell and opened the Bible to Psalm 38. It is the saddest chapter in the entire book. David was crying out to God with such passion.

I lay down on the mattress on the floor of that county jail. Suddenly, I saw the hand of God reaching toward me. I was so desperate, I crawled up into the hand of God and grabbed hold of His finger and wouldn't let go. For three days in that cell, I cried and cried and cried. Others watching me thought I was having a nervous breakdown.

No, I was having a powerful, life-changing encounter with almighty God! I cried until my soul was totally cleaned out.

For almost 23 years, I had run like crazy from God. I went for days and days without ever going home. I traveled out of the country hunting for what I had been searching for. I had had guns held to my head and knives at my throat. I had been robbed. I had been hurt so many times.

I found what I had been seeking when God reached down and picked me up. And to this day, I am still sitting in His hand. He is always faithful to forgive and reach down to help us. He never forsakes us. My life changed when I realized what and who I was, and I fell to my knees crying out to Him.

I went on to finish treatment for my Hepatitis C while in jail. The Hepatitis C went away. In prison, I got into the choir. I was blessing the people. I made a prayer box out of an old shoe box and told everyone that I would pray over any requests every day. They all laughed and made fun of me. One of the inmates had a relative who got very sick. He put his request in the box. After his relative got healed, all of the inmates would put their requests in my box for prayer.

My cell had about thirty people in it. This was a tough prison. They would gather in the corner of the cell every night and fight. Blood flew everywhere. It was horrible. I prayed against the violence continuously.

I read my Bible through and through. I also read every book I could get my hands on.

After a year and a half, they moved me out to a halfway house with six people to a room. While there, the devil attacked. He came back with seven more spirits to torment me. I was having panic attacks and was already on psych meds for anxiety. As I lay on my bed one night, I had a vision. I saw myself going downstairs. Below me, I could see numerous evil spirits and I could smell decaying flesh. It was a vision of hell—demons and death everywhere. I was close to calling the night guard to send me to the psych ward. I thought I was really losing it.

As I lay there, I suddenly felt Jesus nearby—a light shining in the darkness. I never saw His face, but I knew it was Him. Not a word was spoken. His staff whisked through the air, hit the ground, and disintegrated all the evil spirits. No demons, no death, no smells! Nothing left to torment my mind. Only brilliant, glorious light.

This was a major breakthrough in my life. I have no idea how many demons left me that day. I had been delivered!

Before I went to prison, I had built an altar in my home. I was a Universalist. I burned candles and worshiped every kind of idol possible to worship satan. No telling what kind of demons and spirits I had invited into my mind. Those things were tormenting me one last time because satan knew I was soon getting out of that mess.

The staff of Jesus destroyed all the evil forces that were coming against me. I spent another month in that place until I found a place to live in Florida. I had another six months of probation before getting released from the Texas system.

I had bonded with my aunt when I was young. She was a beautiful Christian lady. Even though I hadn't seen her for many years, she allowed me to live with her when I transferred to Florida. My aunt played every Gaither videotape known to man. She also had numerous preaching tapes that ran many hours a day. She was pouring life into me.

I couldn't leave the house or go anywhere. Even though I was in my thirties, I had to be treated like a ten-year-old and learn things all over again. My aunt was determined that I was not going to fall back into my old lifestyle. I couldn't be allowed to be out and about until I had enough confidence and maturity to be a responsible adult. I was still on psych meds for about another five years to control my anxiety and panic attacks.

Being back in Florida was such a blessing. I could see my mom and I worked for my father. I started leading worship at church. I was determined to find my destiny that had been hidden all those years. I never gave up.

My father sent me to Hawaii on a project for him. I believe I ate something bad while in the islands. On the way back to the states, I got violently ill. When I got back, a doctor diagnosed me with severe liver disease. My Hepatitis C had come back with a vengeance.

This was a moment of great trying for me. I fell to my knees and begged God for an answer. "Father, I have done everything You told me to do. Why this?" He was silent.

For the next three years, I got progressively worse. The doctors didn't want to give me any drugs that could further injure my liver. My eyes had already turned yellow. I finally contacted the drug manufacturer for help. They would give me the drugs for free if my doctor would write the prescription and if I would file for disability.

The liver specialist told me the necessary drug would probably kill me. I begged him, "If I don't take this drug, I'm going to die. What is it going to hurt if I take it? I believe it will help me! Please, let me have a chance to live!" He gave his permission and wrote the prescription.

My bloodwork was very abnormal. My symptoms continued. I was passing blood every day and seemed to be getting worse. I couldn't even walk one hundred feet and looked terrible. I was very close to death.

Even before I got sick, I had been leading worship for a children's group at church. During this time, I would drag myself out of bed every Sunday morning and Wednesday night to get to church. As soon as I started singing, God's Holy Ghost power took over. I would walk up and down the aisle singing and praising God. As soon as worship was over, I crawled back to my bed.

The doctor told me I had to continue all medications if I had any hope of survival. I had medications for everything.

Dragging and with God's help, I finished the treatment plan. By that time, I was looking much better.

After waiting two years for my disability claim, I went to see the judge to get his approval. The judge denied my eligibility. I walked out and cried out to God, "What am I going to do now?"

Even though I was confused and hurting, I didn't realize He had a plan bigger than I could imagine. I had zero idea about what He wanted from me or for me.

If you need something, ask Him! He will guide you into your destiny.

In 2010 I went to Haiti a few months after the earthquake. Over a quarter of a million people lost their lives during that catastrophe.

My father builds tents and I was still helping him. I went down to Haiti to help the local churches who were meeting in tents. One night I slept in a hammock near the big tent pitched on the side of the mountain. It was raining so hard that night. Occasionally, I had to climb up to keep the rain from accumulating on the roof.

Hanging on near the top of the tent, I heard this noise that sounded like sheep bleating in the rain. I wondered what kind of animals were making this noise. The squeals got louder and louder.

Suddenly, I realized the noises were coming from children sleeping in the rain on the streets. They were sleeping outside with any kind of protection they could find. At that point, I started crying for them.

I heard God say, "You will have a ministry here in Haiti." I thought I would just a do a few children's church meetings like I had done years earlier. I told a few people what God had said before leaving Haiti. Of course, we all prayed.

Every time I would go home to Florida, I would get another call to set up another tent. This happened several times over the next year and a half. Eventually, I helped churches, businesses, and others get reestablished following the devastation.

A friend called me one night to invite me to Joan Hunter's large ministry meeting. Everyone on the bus was startled because I was the only Caucasian. We went and had a wonderful time.

The next morning, Kelley called me and asked me to sing the next evening. I chose "The More I Seek You, the More I Find You." I was so nervous with thousands of people watching and using different equipment. God was there. I was covered with His peace and everything went great. It was an amazing experience.

During one trip back to the states in early 2012, I laid down one night and had a vision from God. I was sitting in an old wooden boat in the middle of an empty pond. I was painting the birds, the sun, the fish, a house with a chimney, and children fishing on the bank. I am not an artist at all, so this was very interesting.

I asked God, "What does this mean?"

He answered, "Keep painting, David!"

I kept painting. I saw a living spring coming out of and filling the pond. Then the entire picture came alive in front of me. The sun was shining, the kids were playing, the birds were flying, and the boat was now floating in the middle of the pond.

Again, I asked, "What does this mean?"

He said, "You paint your picture and My living water will bring it to life for you."

That was a word from the Lord that I could run with. I knew it was God.

I went home to the U.S. and told my family we were going to start a non-profit ministry and open an orphanage in Haiti. Needless to say, the people who knew me questioned my plan.

A friend from my childhood called me with an invitation to speak at several churches in his area. He flew me to New York, and I shared my vision to the churches we visited. They were fascinated. Before I went home, someone contributed enough money to pay for the upgrades necessary to fix the home I had been staying in when I visited Haiti. The homeowners gave me a price for leasing that three-room home, and the available money was enough to fix everything.

At our home church in Lakeland, a plumber walked up to me the first Sunday I was home from New York. He said, "God has spoken to me. I am supposed to fix bathrooms for your home in Haiti!" He did not know anything about our plans.

I had filed the certificate for licensing several months before. The license was approved within eight months. Other homes are still waiting for their license after many years.

The home was prepared and we interviewed the first three children in October. A lady was trying to help abandoned children. She had about 20 kids in two small rooms. I found the necessary social worker and I picked up the first three Haitian children on December 31, 2012.

We signed the papers, loaded them up, and took them home. The electricity hadn't been turned on yet, and I had only a few hundred dollars in my pocket. We all walked to the neighborhood church the first night, which was January 1, 2013, and the pastor prayed over them. When I told the local church about the orphanage, the people laughed at me.

God brought another three children and another and another. We ended up with many boys from 18 months to 12 years of age. One of the older boys now works for me at the Black and White for Jesus Children's Home.

God's Holy Spirit knows His plans for us. He is with me every step of the way to fulfill God's vision for me. I must have faith, pray, work, and follow His direction. And I am still painting the picture. I am so amazed that God has brought it all to life in front of my eyes.

A visitor came and donated enough money for the down payment to buy the house. Others came and helped pay for some land. The boy's home grew and the home was purchased. God spoke to me again. He wanted another home for girls that adjoined the boys' home. Several years later, a word came to establish a home for special needs children. In the last eight years, we have grown to 67 children between the three homes. It is amazing what God has done.

Several years passed. Joan Hunter came back to Haiti on a missions trip for meetings. I always wanted to go to Israel. She had posted the information about the scheduled trip. Under her post, I added, "I would certainly like to go to Israel someday." Some friends were going with her to Israel and read that post. They knew a little about my history and paid my way to Israel.

Joan had asked me if I wanted to be ordained. Of course I did, but the time wasn't right at that time. A couple years ago, I was able to get all the necessary materials to study. The Lord opened the door for me to go to Houston, Texas and go through the ordination meetings. Praise God! I am now ordained!

God has continued to expand my vision for Haiti. He is still painting my picture. I am looking forward to bigger and better. I know He will supply the funds necessary to purchase the home for the girls and the special needs home. We have plans for a school and cafeteria.

It's amazing. Sixty-seven children call me "Daddy." Imagine, this person who was such a mess is now Daddy to all these kids.

I was nothing. I can only give Him glory for what He has done in my life and what He is continuing to do as I continue to paint my picture.

Even though I couldn't understand that God was blessing me during all of my skirmishes and misadventures, today I can see His blessings and His hand upon me even back to my teenage years.

He picked up the broken pieces of my life and He made something beautiful out of nothing.

God bless you!

David Wine

Haiti

wineinchrist@yahoo.com

Chapter Four

A MOTHER'S DREAM

D'Onna Winn was at one of my meetings in 1985 shortly after she and her husband were married. I gave her a word from the Lord that she was going to have a son. Shortly after being given this prophetic word, D'Onna had written the name Seth in her Bible in remembrance of the prophetic word she had received.

She went on to have three daughters. I'm so glad they didn't choose to stone the prophet like they did in the Bible.

At age 47, D'Onna wasn't feeling well, so she went to the doctor. She was told that she was pregnant! She was shocked beyond words! She and her husband weren't on good terms, but she did remember they'd been intimate one time during that season.

D'Onna held on to her dream and did not let it die. A few months after that, their son, Seth, was born. He has been a pure delight to them.

I want to encourage you to never give up on your dreams. Delight yourself in the Lord and He will give you the desires and secret petitions of your heart!

Chapter Five

HOW LONG, LORD?

In 2009, I had just turned 23 and was so excited to marry Emmanuel, my best friend and the love of my life. September 26, 2009 was a beautiful, warm, and sunny day. I was gifted a gorgeous earring and necklace set by a family friend. It wasn't anything extravagant, but it was so special to me. The large, super-sparkly moissanite stones were set in sterling silver, and I knew I would treasure the set forever.

In the days following our wedding, Emmanuel and I stayed a couple nights in a beautiful hotel in Albuquerque and visited the local aquarium and zoo. While getting ready to sightsee during our honeymoon, I realized I could not find one of the earrings to complete my wedding set. As I frantically searched, I asked myself, "What kind of new bride loses part of her wedding set?" I was so distraught. I prayed so hard for the Holy Spirit to show me where I had misplaced it. As a diehard romantic, my heart sank as I knew the odds of ever finding that lost earring were slim to none. I would never be able to share the set with my future daughter or daughter-in-law. I had failed. It was lost. I held out hope I would find it even until we checked out of the hotel; however, I still had not found it.

My failure was so tangible, I don't remember ever saying a word to anyone of the lost jewel. After lots of praying, lots of tears and knots in my stomach, I safely stored the necklace and single earring in a box in my jewelry drawer—overcome with the knowledge it would never be whole again. Every time I would clean out my jewelry drawer, I would come across this broken set and dread would rise up inside me again. And each time, I would tuck it away again.

Fast forward through the years. It was the week of our tenth wedding anniversary. I was walking through my mother-in-law's house when something glittery caught my eye. My mother-in-law is a pastor and frequently organizes what we call "Café de Mujeres" or a women's café. She always has gems around the house that she uses as decoration at church. I honestly thought this glittery jewel was one of her many decorations. This jewel had been sitting on her coffee table for quite some time. I would notice it and brush it off. But during the week of our anniversary, I was compelled to investigate.

As I approached the jewel, a wave of familiarity and utter joy swept over me as I realized, in disbelief, this was my lost earring.

I don't think anyone could imagine my absolute and utter joy when I picked up this jewel and recognized it immediately. *It was my lost earring!* I couldn't believe it. I ran to find Mery to ask her where she had found it. I couldn't talk fast enough. Thankfully, she understood my question. She simply told me she had found it in the rubber seal inside her washing machine.

In the early days of our marriage, Emmanuel and I lived in an apartment building that only had a laundromat, so we opted to wash clothes at Mery's house. The only explanation I have for this is that my lost earring must have been in the bag I thought I had inspected thoroughly. When we washed said bag, it became lodged in her washer, and for *ten years* was stuck, snug and safe, in the lining of her washing machine.

I was dumbfounded. But most of all I was loved. Loved by a heavenly Father who knew my heart's desire was to have a complete wedding set. Loved by a Father who had taken care of that piece of jewelry for all those years. It was so significant to me that I would find it the week of our tenth anniversary. It just doesn't get any better. He is the ultimate storyteller and the ultimate Father who shows us His extravagant love in the simplest of ways. I am loved by the God who sees me (see Gen. 16:13).

Fallon Davila

Fallon.davila09@gmail.com

Chapter Six

BEAUTY FOR ASHES

By the grace of God, I was set free from a 15-year drug addiction in September of 2008. I started smoking crack in 1994, a few months after I had gotten my nursing license. I was 19 years old with a two-year-old daughter, and I was very excited about my future.

Within a few months of starting this drug, I quit my job as a nurse and lost everything, including my daughter. I was on the streets doing whatever it took to get my drugs, no matter how dangerous or demeaning. I didn't care about myself or anyone else. All I cared about was my next high. The next 15 years of my life were pure hell. Satan set out to destroy me and did everything in his power to do so.

I was consistently in and out of jail and rehab. I finally gave up on rehab, but I continued to go to jail over and over again. I ended up with twenty-two misdemeanors and three felony convictions. I know I was arrested over fifty times and I spent a total of about six years of my life in different jails and prisons.

I lived through numerous near-death experiences on the streets. Many girls I knew along the way did lose their lives. Once, I actually died on a shot of cocaine, but by grace the drug addicts who were with me were able to revive me with CPR and a little "divine intervention."

Thank God, I had a praying mom who helped keep me alive long enough to receive my deliverance! No matter how bad things seemed in the natural, she never gave up hope that God could and would set me free. Friends and family members would tell her again and again that I was a lost cause, yet she still refused to give up on me. She faithfully continued to pray and decree freedom over my life until we got breakthrough.

Along the way I had two more daughters, giving birth to one of them while incarcerated. I just couldn't seem to get it together, even for them. My mom and ex-husband ended up raising my daughters for me. I was consumed with shame and guilt over not being the mother they needed and deserved, yet this guilt and shame was all a part of the destructive cycle that was keeping me trapped.

I had given my heart to God as a child, so every time I went to jail, I would run back to Him for comfort, but I never truly surrendered my will and my life to Him. So every time I would get out of jail, I would eventually, if not immediately, go back to the drugs.

After struggling through this nightmare cycle of self-destruction for 15 years, I finally realized that I could not just give God little pieces of my life and expect to receive freedom from my addiction. I understood that in order for Him to bring me freedom, I was going to have to surrender my life to Him 100 percent. I also knew there would be many steps I would have to take to walk out my deliverance.

In September of 2008, I was again facing criminal charges that should have gotten me years in prison. Around that same time, my mom had told me about a Christian restoration program out in Arizona for women like me. It was a part of Patricia King Ministries. They would take in one woman at a time and teach her how to build a Christ-centered life as she walked through healing and deliverance. I was finally sick and tired of being sick and tired and I agreed to go if they would accept me. Thank God, I was chosen for this program!

I rededicated my life to God, and this time I laid it all down, holding nothing back. I was truly hungry for the restoration only God can bring. I was also finally able to forgive myself and leave all of my shame and guilt at the feet of Jesus.

While I was in this nine-month program called "Restor8ion House," God began to speak to me about reaching the people I had left behind who were still trapped in their addictions. He told me to start writing down everything I was learning that was bringing me freedom and to put it into a book that He would help me get out to many. It would be like a map so they could follow me out of the chains of addiction!

So, during my first year clean, I wrote *Walk It Out*. It is a 90-day devotional on freedom from addiction. So far, we have been able to get over ten thousand copies into different jails and prisons across the United States. What a blessing it is that everything my family and I went through is now being used for good!

I stayed in Arizona and worked for Patricia King Ministries for the next nine years. It was such an amazing time in my life. I prayed and believed God to restore the relationships with my three daughters and send me a good Christian husband. I heard God tell me that He would restore those relationships and that I would have another child. At the time, that was a huge promise to me because my tubes had been tied ten years after the birth of my youngest daughter in 1998, and I was 35 years old.

My girls had been hurt and disappointed by me over and over for years, so trust didn't come overnight, but I never gave up. I just continued to pray, decree, and show them how much I loved them. One by one, God has continued to work miracles of restoration in these relationships.

Now I will admit, trusting God for a husband wasn't the easiest thing I have ever had to do as a Christian woman. I felt like I had already lost so many years and I wanted that special man to come quickly. I prayed and decreed and continued to walk with God and believe that He would send me the right man at the right time.

I went on several "first dates" with some men who definitely were not it! Let me be honest here, I was not patient about this at all—but I didn't give up. I knew God would be faithful and keep His promise to me. He had already done so many miracles in my life, so my faith had grown exponentially. Then in the fall of 2012, I met my amazing husband and we knew within weeks that God had brought us together. We were married within four months, and this year we will celebrate eight years of marriage.

My husband did not have any children so I shared with him before we married that my tubes had been tied. I believed God would give us a baby and there were several options we could try. He said he loved me and wanted me with or without kids.

I was almost 39 when we married. There were many challenges and we suffered several losses, but I refused to give up. I knew I had heard from God on this so I pressed in for our miracle. Through a series of supernatural miracles and prayers from Patricia King and Joan Hunter, I got pregnant with twins. In February of 2016, I gave birth to full term twins—a boy and a girl. They are perfect in every way.

In the last twelve years since I was set free from drug addiction, God has blessed my life more than I ever could have imagined. I am so grateful for all He has done and especially thankful that I had a praying mom who never gave up on me and continued to believe for my freedom until we got the victory! If you are believing for yourself or a loved one to be set free from any type of bondage, *never give up!*

I was the worst of the worst, and if He can do it for me, He can do it for anyone!

Ginger Brown

President of Walk it Out Ministries

walkitoutministries.com

https://www.facebook.com/gingerwalkitout

Chapter Seven

BEAUTY IN THE MAKING

I will never forget the day I decided I wanted to compete for the title of Miss America. Even though my big sister had won Miss Chicago, Miss Illinois, and was the first runner-up to Miss America, I had never done a pageant in my life! I remember being twelve, watching her get all dolled up in glitzy gowns, hair, and make-up. I grew up as a tomboy jock whose life revolved 24/7 around being a volleyball player. Here I was, now age 23, with just one year of eligibility, one chance, to compete for the coveted crown.

Fearful thoughts bombarded my mind: "You don't even know how to put on make-up! When was the last time you wore heels? You have to perform in front of people! You are shy! What will your friends think? Other girls have more experience. They've done this for years! You're not going to fit in. What if you don't win? You're going to look so stupid!"

The fear was nearly paralyzing. I found myself in tears and anxious at just the thought of telling my loved ones. For weeks I kept my idea a secret, but every day I would watch videos of old Miss America pageants for motivation. My excitement and courage began to build. I saw what outstanding role models the contestants were! I saw them empowering kids around the nation and speaking on important topics. I saw them using the scholarship money they won to better their education, and I read about how successful they became as business women, doctors, lawyers, and non-profit leaders. I was sufficiently impressed and inspired!

I wanted to have this incredible experience for myself, but I knew that saying "yes" to this dream would require me to get completely out of my comfort zone. I just couldn't muster up the courage to give God my "yes" at first. For months, I wrestled with the call. I tried to ignore it. When I couldn't ignore it, I tried to edit it. I wanted out!

God always knows what His children need. Every Sunday leading up to the pageant, it was as if my pastor was speaking directly to me. I left encouraged and convicted to truly believe that I was a daughter of destiny, a history maker, and a queen! I left every service believing I could do this! One Sunday, I had even successfully talked myself out of competing when my pastor stepped up to the pulpit to preach his sermon, entitled "Just Do It!" That message stopped me dead in my tracks as he preached about operating in bold obedience and answering the call.

I knew right then I had to make a choice: Was I going to let my fear or my passion fuel this decision in my life? I could walk away and be comfortable or I could sprint toward my dream.

That Sunday, I said "yes" to God's dream for me and He gave me the strength to get started! From that moment, things shifted. He overwhelmed me with a supernatural confidence and boldness that propelled me throughout the training.

My sister began coaching me on how to walk in an evening gown, deliver a compelling interview, and captivate an audience with my stage presence. Pageant night would be the first time I ever sang a solo in public, so I began taking voice lessons. I was used to singing in the back pews of the choir, but now I would have no choice but to sing center stage.

As I kept praying, practicing, and preparing, my confidence grew. I learned to trust God with my weaknesses and let Him make my crooked places straight. I knew if I could give my best, God would do the rest!

Three months later, He did just that! I stepped on the stage and God showed up! One unforgettable November evening, I won the first pageant of my life and walked away with the title of Miss Houston 2014. I also won the Talent

Award for singing, the Interview Award, and the People's Choice Award! Not a bad start for a rookie competitor!

The truth is: God knows us better than we know ourselves. He knows the gifts, the talents, and greatness He has stored up inside of us, but it's our responsibility to take the first step. More often than not, our first step leads to even greater things ahead.

Since then, God has expanded my platform to inspire thousands of girls around the country. Since performing my first solo that night, I've performed the National Anthem for the Houston Rockets and the Houston Astros twice. Only God can take a girl who was too shy to perform in front of one person and put her in front of forty thousand. Only God can do that!

Now I know firsthand that when God gives us audacious dreams, we don't have to have it all figured out. We don't have to be equipped in the natural. When we push past fears and dare to trust God, there are experiences of a lifetime and opportunities to bring God glory on the other side. Indeed, with God all things are possible (see Matt. 19:26)!

Isis Smalls

Miss Houston 2014

National Empowerment Speaker

Amazon Bestselling Author

www.isissmalls.com

management@isissmalls.com

Chapter Eight

HOPE IN THE WAITING

God gave me a story and branded me with hope. I am forever changed.

"Was it about being pregnant or about being a mother?" This was the question I asked myself in the middle of this chapter of our story. In September of 2015, Adam and I had been married one year. Because we were a little older than the norm, we did not want to wait too long to start our family.

It took nine months to get our first positive pregnancy test. I remember the thrill of getting that first line. We celebrated it, but after a couple of days of taking tests the line did not progress into a thicker and darker one, as it should have. The baby did not stay. I was still vibrant with excitement and had no idea I would log years in the waiting room.

About a year into trying, my doctor put me on progesterone and then Clomid for a while. The medications made me feel a bit deranged, but I was willing to try these things to help a baby stay.

After nothing was working, we soon took it a step further and decided to try an intrauterine insemination. That is a procedure to help place the sperm directly into the uterus during ovulation. Over time, we ended up doing four of those rounds. Strangely enough, all of these failed. During some of them, I was able to get pregnant but the same pattern was happening—the babies were not fully implanting into the uterus.

Within two years, I had been pregnant six times. The longing for a child was a deep, primal need, and being unable to carry a pregnancy to term was devastating. There was pain and shame. It seemed socially unacceptable. In some settings, I even found myself "window shopping" for that pregnancy glow.

In January of 2017, the Lord spoke to me through a song from one of my favorite worship artists. It was a song about keeping your heart open. That year, Adam and I fought to do just that. Our word was *open*. Anytime we would face another loss, we were determined to keep our hearts open.

What does that look like to keep a heart open? For me, I celebrated every pink line on the pregnancy tests even though I wasn't sure if the baby would stay. It was a risk, but isn't that what faith is? Also, the language used around our home was as if I was going to carry the baby full term. In Jesus' strength, we praised Him. When hesitation reared its head, we kept pressing into hope. Along the journey, there were parts of Him I don't think I fully knew. The walls of my heart were being stretched and expanded. It's hard to even put into words, but my reach became so desperate.

The spirit of comparison tried to befriend me. In order to steer clear from this poison, I made the decision to defy it. I chose to celebrate and bless every woman around me who became pregnant. It wasn't always easy, but I had an awareness that my children would be born on this earth at a specific time. I knew God had an appointed time for our babies to be born.

That thought kept me going! In the foggy moments, I remembered just that. I was diligent to not give up and not give in to the victim mentality. I chose not to be envious or jealous but truly celebrate each story. Giving gifts, hugs, and showing up in their celebration was key. Dear reader, if you are in that place of comparison, I encourage you to find someone who is celebrating the thing you are waiting for and show up for them.

In 2016, I decided to purchase a tangible item that I could look at every day to remind me that at some point I would be a mom. In faith, I bought a diaper bag. It hung on the doorknob in our future nursery. It was another reminder to not give up, to stay steady and be strong. We went in that room quite often to worship and pray. Every time I saw the diaper bag, it seemed to whisper, "I will be filled one day." I always thought faith was a one-time decision, but I started noticing it was a lifetime unfolding.

There was a diagnosis. In June of 2017, we finally figured out what was happening with my body. I had a higher level of white blood cells or what they call "killer cells." The cells would see my babies as foreign invaders or cancer and kill them off.

Praise God for doctors and medicine. Our fertility doctor mentioned that IVF would be the best route to take because it was about timing. He would administer a specific drug that would help lower the cells right before putting the embryos in. It sounded hopeful, but we wanted to take a month off and pray about it. I secretly thought that going through treatment would fix everything and we would finally be parents, but I still had to surrender in the waiting. I still had to trust God to do it.

Thanksgiving re-patterned our thinking. During this time, our hearts developed a steadiness. Our church community had done this well, and we had learned so much about centering ourselves around one thing—the man Jesus. We thanked Him that our bodies worked, we thanked Him for what He had already done in our lives, and we thanked Him for our future babies over and over again. This alone set our hearts on a heavenly perspective.

July 2017 was a wild ride. Faith got a little bolder. My husband and I purchased a family car! The funny thing was, the week we bought it I found out that I was pregnant. I remember buying Adam a mug, and in the bottom it said, "You're a daddy." I was not on any medications. That month we were in the middle of rest. It was the longest I had carried!

But I was not expecting what took place next. On that July Monday morning, I could barely breathe. I got up just like any normal Monday to go pee. What came out in the toilet was a complete shock. I tried to quickly reason in my mind that some women bleed during pregnancy, but that wasn't working. Anxiety rose. I called the nurse immediately and set up an appointment.

The next twenty-four hours of waiting for that appointment were torture. By Tuesday, they drew my blood. I got a call Wednesday morning. The HCG numbers were dropping. Everything in me seemed to scream. "Please, Lord, let this baby stay!" We warred and prayed. It was devastating. The worst of it was I had to keep going back to the office to do blood draws so they could make sure my body was doing what it was supposed to do. It was the darkest time of the entire journey. The baby didn't make it. My heart was broken.

Our pastor had recently given a great revelation about when you face a day of trouble. Now here I was getting to exercise that message. My day of trouble was here. I gave myself a few days to lay low, feel the emotions, get raw and real with the Lord. I knew it wasn't a place anyone else could go with me. Jesus was like a warm blanket wrapped around me, comforting me, and was with me in it.

One night during that week I woke up around two in the morning to the sound of someone saying my name at the end of my bed. It scared the fire out of me. In my heart, I felt it was Jesus. This was the first audible voice I had heard thus far, and all He said was my name. I knew He was with me and that was enough. The next morning, I felt so much peace.

As the week went on, I set a goal. I told myself after seven days I would move forward. It didn't mean I couldn't cry or have weak moments, but that I would not allow myself to stay in that place. I remember thinking that dark place wouldn't lead me anywhere good. It was so sweet of the Lord to lead me gently so that I would not give up.

The end of that week was a detail for the books! Adam made me breakfast that Friday morning. He said, "Jev, I had an old company that dissolved and I am getting money back from it next week." He said the amount and my jaw dropped open. It was exactly what we needed to move forward with the IVF procedure.

We felt so much peace and decided to go through with it. Another glimmer of hope was shining. It was like a stepping stone to the next piece of our puzzle. Hope was an invitation into the unseen that required the truth about who God was. Against all odds, the unseen is what became more real than our eyes could perceive.

From the end of August to November, there were needles, meds, sonograms, doctor visits, prayers, tears, anxiety, declarations, anticipation, excitement, and fears all infused within. All of the prep work led to an egg retrieval. The doctor needed my body to be in a specific place to extract the eggs. I was enlightened on all the things that needed to line up in order for a woman to conceive a baby. It's truly a miraculous event.

November 8, 2017 was the day. My doctor was able to retrieve ten eggs! We were praising God that we had gotten ten! After that, the embryologist mixed Adam's sperm with each egg, and out of the ten we got six embryos. They froze the embryos for a couple of months. January 8, 2018, a nurse came to my house to give me an IV medication to lower the blood cells.

Two days later, I was excited and ready to put the two babies inside me—one boy and one girl! Implanting two increased the chances of one staying. Now for the hardest part, the two-week wait! If you are a woman and have tried to conceive on any level, then you know about the two-week wait! It's daunting! There is nothing you can do to speed up the process.

Everything in me wanted to take lots of pregnancy tests, but there was no point. We had our community and family praying big prayers, standing in agreement with us. We had faith that one or both babies would stay! The day came and I got another positive! But just like other times, the positive pregnancy test did not progress into dark, thick lines. My heart sank. The energy, time, effort, pain, and sacrifice it took to go through the process was not for the faint of heart.

When I close my eyes and think about that part of the story, I still get emotional. There was desperation in me that was willing to do anything to carry a baby full term. *Anything!* At this point in the story, it would have been so easy to just give up. It was harder to stay present. Call it my makeup, my upbringing, the fighter in me, or just Jesus, but I was not going to quit. I was determined to be a mother.

Several weeks later, I was getting ready to share a message at a women's retreat. It was my first time to ever speak in front of women. I was honestly ready to throw in the towel and not teach at the women's event. I was sitting with Holy Spirit one day and felt Him whisper, "Will you let Me use you in your pain?"

Without thinking, I responded, "Yes." I pushed forward. I actually told my infertility story and what I was dealing with for the first time, publicly. The power of God showed up. Many women could not believe I was sharing in the middle of my journey with no signs of a baby. He used me in my weakness. All I did was show up. If you find yourself weak, that's the best place to be. Find ways He can use you now.

Our perspective of Him was not being altered. This circumstance wasn't shaping us. We were slowly being fashioned, rearranged, and realigned with Jesus as He changed us. After dusting ourselves off and resting a couple of months, we were ready to try another round of IVF. I even left my job as a preschool director so that my body could rest and not deal with any kind of stress.

The week I was leaving my job, a couple of interesting things happened. First, the church leadership asked me if I wanted to become the women's pastor. See, even though I was longing for a child and going through the ups and downs of that, I was alive on the inside. God had done a work in me. Over the course of time, my pain turned into purpose. My longing was not just for the promise but for the Promise Keeper. I humbly said, "Yes." Right in the middle of what I thought was a barren season, God was showing me fruit. The fruit I was bearing had led to promotion. It's amazing! When my eyes were fixed on Him, He showed me there was so much more waiting for me.

Renewing my mind was vital. I think of a picture of a garden. When I renewed my mind with His Word, God pruned, watered, and caused rebirth to happen. Even seeds that were sown in past seasons were growing. I was fruitful even though my womb was still barren. I prayed scriptures and held on to the Word of God. It kept me from hardening my heart and allowed me to stay soft before Him.

Stories like Hannah were comforting. In the middle of her pain she was misunderstood, humble, faithful, satisfied, committed, and at peace. Oh, how I gleaned from her. Other scriptures throughout the Word gave me permission to release, let go, and be free.

One verse Adam and I listened to repeatedly was Galatians 6:9, which says, "Let us not become weary in doing good, for at the proper time we will reap a harvest if we do not give up" (NIV). We were set on not giving up. It didn't mean we couldn't cry, show anger, have meltdowns, and fall down. It just meant that no matter the pain, we would get back up. We were a team and knew where to fix our gaze.

Going back for my last week as a preschool director, a second thing happened. The Holy Spirit highlighted something and I could not let it go. An old co-worker showed up at the school and was considering putting her child in our program. I hadn't seen her in a while. We caught up and it turned out that she adopted her daughter a couple of years previously. She told me about the agency she used, and I put it in the back of my mind.

The following week, I was ready for the IVF procedure. The doctor put in another boy and a girl. I told Adam I needed a plan moving forward if these babies didn't stay. We agreed that adoption would be it. Having children was always in our hearts and adoption felt like a good next step.

During this round of IVF, we had what felt like the masses praying for us and believing with us that these babies would stay. Going into the procedure, our faith was strong. Another pregnancy did happen and, yet again, it ended in another loss.

Our individual healings were a process, different from each other. We gave each other so much grace and stayed connected. I know marriages have split up over infertility, and we wanted to choose His storyline over us. Another song lyric that I'll insert here from my favorite songwriter is "Help is a person, hope is a man, there's nothing too big enough for you, you always have a plan." These words were healing to my soul. Hope had a plan!

Now, you may remember we were given the money for IVF. Questions rose in my heart because there was no fruit from this experience. Why wasn't it clear? Why didn't we see the fruit? Wasn't the money from God? So many questions! What I came to realize was that those questions never brought me clear vision. They only made things cloudy. No, I still don't know the answers, but it was okay to ask. I didn't stay there long because sitting in that place could have led me down a different path that wasn't doused with hope.

In May of 2018, we felt a shift. The Lord was leading us toward adoption. It was time to pursue it. We chose the agency my old co-worker told me about and began raising funds. Our family and community helped us sell t-shirts and put together a garage sale and a pop-up store. We were blown away!

Mother's Day of 2018 will forever be a memory etched in our hearts. An anonymous donor put $24,000 in the offering basket at church on behalf of our adoption process. We were shocked! God was revealing Himself as an extravagant giver. It was uncomfortable. Never in my life had I received a financial blessing like this.

By August of 2018, we were officially a waiting family and we were fully funded. That is rare! A miracle. At any point, we could be chosen to be parents. This was another journey in itself. Birth moms were able to look at our profile through the agency and choose. There was still more waiting, but I could see that Jesus was doing more in me during my waiting than any place else. I could see rays of color, beams of light, and a sweet fragrance was in the air. My patience seemed stronger than before.

Declaration was a powerful tool amid uncertainty. Did you know you have the power to change your circumstance instead of your circumstance changing you? James 3 talks about the tongue. Romans 4 says we can call things into being that do not exist. I could go on and on about how powerful our words are and what they create.

There were days I would declare peace over myself. There were days I declared Psalm 113:9 and made it personal: "I will be a happy mother of children," or declared from Psalm 127, "Our quiver will be full." I am a woman of declaration, and I believe it is a big deal to God. The funny thing was as I was making these declarations and calling our babies forth, Jesus snuck up on me. Suddenly, my eyes were so full of light and my hunger for Him increased. It was actually out of His strength that I was able to declare.

July 2018 was another piece to our story. I remember running into Joan Hunter after a session at WOFL, a women's conference. My dear friend introduced us and I told Joan a piece of my story and where I was at in that particular season. She prayed over me and boldly declared that I would have a baby in my womb by July 2019, one year later, and that I would carry full term. When she said that, it bore witness in my spirit. I believed what God was saying through her and knew this was going to happen.

Sometimes, we need others to declare and decree over us, to prophesy and believe with us. I left that conference on fire for the Lord knowing He would give me the desire of my heart.

From August to January, we had several birth moms choose us in their top two selections, but they would always go with the other family. Yet again, Adam and I clung to hope. In the middle of the adoption chapter, I decided to get my body healthy by taking vitamins, exercising, and I even saw an herbalist. She noticed my blood levels were off and gave me natural drops to help normalize them. This was all toward getting pregnant eventually, not knowing the timing.

On February 7, 2019 we were eagerly awaiting a call. The pregnancy counselor, Lindsay (from the agency), told us a birth mom would be viewing our profile that day. Around 4:45 P.M. we had not heard anything. We decided to take communion and meet with Him at the table. This detail is a pearl in my heart. We invited Him to sit with us and prayed that if this birth mom was meant to choose us, then the door would be wide open. An hour later, we just knew the birth mom chose someone else.

But 6:33 P.M. came and it was the call of our lives! Lindsay said, "She chose you!" Followed by jumping up and down and lots of screams—we were elated. After viewing seven other families that day, we were the last ones she looked at. She saw a few pages of our book and told the counselor she didn't need to keep viewing our profile—that we were the ones. She chose us. We were finally going to be parents!

When we saw that little face that looked nothing like us for the first time, it was a holy moment. We began to realize that if God had not spent that extra time on us, shaping us, molding us, and awakening us, we would not be holding our baby and being asked to be her parents. We would not have known that the disappointment of experiencing losses month after month could become the most beautiful thing we have ever seen. Had the other pregnancies stuck, she would have never been our little miracle. It changed us.

The crazy part was God was not done yet. Exactly eleven days after our baby girl was born, we found out we were pregnant! Now remember, there was history in past pregnancies, but I remember vividly the Holy Spirit whispering, "This one will stay." That Saturday morning, March 2, 2019, I ran out into the kitchen waiving the pregnancy test above my head screaming, crying, and laughing all at the same time. "Babe, I'm pregnant, I'm pregnant!" The embrace felt like Christmas morning. Tears filled our eyes. God did it! Nine months later, our little miracle boy came at the most perfect time.

For me, it was about motherhood and I was willing to step into it however it looked. The amazing part is that it turned out better than we could think, ask, or imagine! Looking back, I see clearly what He authored in my waiting. He branded me with hope and hope always multiplies.

And there is more—we started a company called Hope Bag. We are selling diaper bags to current and future mamas to be. Our mission is to spread hope, encourage those in the waiting, and give back ten percent of each purchase to a family who is going through adoption. It has been so beautiful to see where God is taking us with our story.

If you are in the place of waiting and longing, *do not give up*. He is not finished with your story yet. If you want encouragement and support, find me at www.hopebag.co. I would love to champion you on your journey.

Jevanna Cherrington

hello@hopebag.co

www.hopebag.co

Instagram: hopebag.co

Facebook: The Hope Bag

Chapter Nine

WORSHIP TO THE WHITE HOUSE

Some would say that it's not always about the final destination but it's the journey that gets you to that place. At the time of this story, I am still a fairly young man (36 years young), married to the woman of my dreams, and have four beautiful children. I grew up in the small town of Greenville, Texas where I was a worship leader by the age of ten. Full-time ministry and music have been my life since I can remember, but that changed around 2014.

I was leading worship at a Joan Hunter conference near Houston, Texas, and my good friend Lisa was the official photographer. She randomly (not so random) mentioned to me that I should look into becoming a photographer. At the time, I probably laughed at her and said something like, "You're crazy." Remember, I'd always been a musician and worship leader, so changing my "profession" wasn't even a thought. Lisa handed me her camera during one of the messages and told me to take a few pictures. I did, and it was love at first snap.

Lisa had told me to pray about getting into photography. More specifically, she told me to look into political photography. Now, I knew she was really insane because I didn't even like politics at the time; however, I told her I'd pray about it. After I returned home to the Phoenix area, I began to ask God what it was all about. I felt like He gave me the green light to begin looking into political photography.

My wife, Kylie, started attending a local Bible study, and by divine appointment our state senator's wife attended the same group. Kylie mentioned that I was trying to get into photography and that I should connect with Senator

Steve Smith. I called him and told him my story and that I was trying to get some experience in photography. He was gracious enough to invite me to the state capitol to take some photos.

About a month or two into learning about photography, the Lord woke me up with the words, "You'll be the chief photographer at the White House someday."

I literally responded with, "What is that?" I got out of bed and did what anyone would do who had just heard the Lord tell them something they didn't know anything about—I Googled it.

Jesus knew what He was talking about because that is a position at the White House. As you could imagine, I was super excited to hear those words. But then I started to think, "Wait…I don't have a degree in photo-journalism. I don't have any contacts in DC. I don't even have professional gear."

My mind started racing, but He quickly calmed me down and told me to take one step at a time. He gave me a decree to make every day. I obeyed. As I dropped my kids off at school, I would decree this:

- I will be the nation's leading political photographer and will teach many the intricate details of capturing the best moments of their candidate.

- I will be wealthy and full of wisdom to take care of my family, the poor, and needy.

- My businesses are extremely blessed and favored!

- I will be the chief photographer for the President of the United States and serve my country with honor.

- I will assist those willing to put in the time and work to reach their goals and dreams even if it's going further and faster than I have gone.

One of my mentors, Patricia King, once told me that when God gives you a vision, create a vision board with the things that you need to accomplish it. I had never created a vision board before, but I felt like I was supposed to do this. I knew what equipment I needed, but I didn't have the resources to purchase it. I printed exactly what

I wanted on a piece a paper and hung it in my office. Every time I looked up from my computer, I saw it hanging there and would pray that God would provide.

One night I was on Facebook when I received a message from a dear friend who had followed our worship ministry. She said that God told her to sow into what God had coming for us. She asked me if I had PayPal. I sent her my PayPal information by email. She messaged me back shortly and asked if I received the gift. I had not received it so she tried again. After the second failed attempt, she said she would call PayPal directly.

As she talked with PayPal, all three transactions went through! I quickly messaged her and told her that there was a mistake. She said she would take care of it. A few minutes later, she messaged me and said the Lord told her to give it all. Are you ready for this? It was *exactly* what I needed to purchase everything on my vision board! Just thinking about that moment as I type makes me want to give God a big *shout!*

The Lord began to connect me strategically and sovereignly with people all over the nation who would help me get one step closer to fulfilling this new call on my life. I was quickly hired to photograph a statewide senate campaign, many local events, as well as become connected with some of the top conservative political voices in our nation.

If anyone knows me, they know I'm very active on social media and post a lot of my journey there. I was able to connect with one of the White House photographers on Instagram, and she began to follow my work. After a little over a year of watching my work, she reached out to me and said that the office of the Vice President was looking to hire a photo editor and would I be interested. In the words of my good friend Joan Hunter, "Let me pray about it, umm, *yes*." I applied for the job, and within a month they hired me!

That was the next step in my journey. God has had His hand on this from the very beginning. Even though I've worked hard to learn this new craft, I know it was only God who could have orchestrated this beautiful testimony. It hasn't been all roses and there have been many difficult situations along the way, but I know we are in the will of God and He hasn't failed us yet.

Every day as I get the opportunity to walk into the gates of the White House, I begin to pray over our President, Vice President, elected leaders, and the entire nation. I walk the halls of the West Wing and release God's wisdom, peace, and favor. I'm absolutely amazed and eternally grateful for what God has entrusted us with. Even when this chapter comes to a close, I know that God's purposes will remain. Never give up and always be ready for God to do a miracle in your life and the life of those you encounter.

Jonathan Williams

Photographer, Worship Leader, and Minister
Web www.politicalshoots.com
www.linkedin.com/in/politicalshoots
IG & Twitter @politicalshoots
Facebook @officialjonathanwilliams

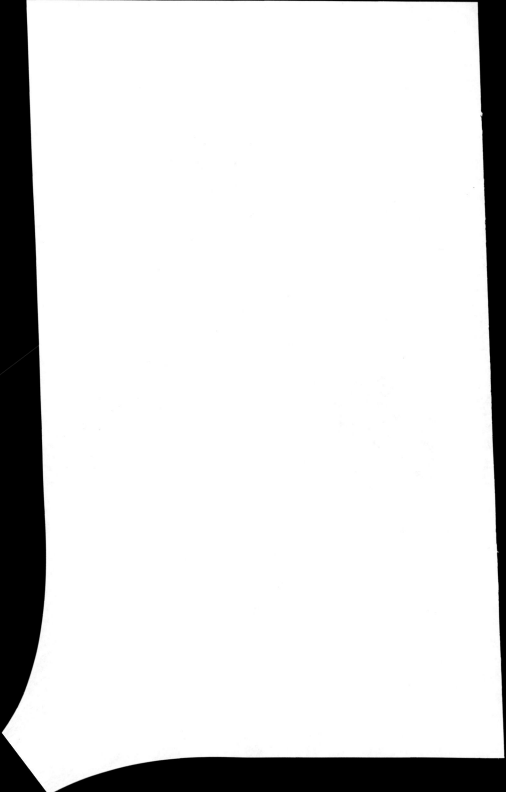

Chapter Ten

BREAKING THE SPIRIT OF POVERTY

Years ago, I developed a very toxic relationship that began to take over my life and marriage. I am not very proud of this relationship. It affected where we lived, where we went to school, the type of vehicle we drove (or whether or not I bought a vehicle), and even when and where we went on vacation.

To be honest, I was not even aware of how deeply entangled I was. It was if I had a mental block in this area that kept me from seeing the truth of just how detrimental it was. This toxic relationship was with none other than the spirit of poverty. That's right! I was bound by a spirit of poverty and didn't even realize it.

What do I mean by a spirit of poverty? The simple definition of poverty is the state of being extremely poor or the state of being inferior in quality or insufficient in amount. By that definition alone, I was in poverty. But the truth is that poverty is much more. Poverty deals with the inability to recognize, receive, and walk in the abundance of God. It is not only to operate in lack, but it is also the inability to recognize the value of what you already possess.

My friends, make no mistake. Poverty is more than an economic condition; it is a mindset and spiritual force that keeps a person or group of people from operating in the plan and purpose of God for their lives. You see, God is unlimited in everything, so lack is not a part of His Kingdom.

Unfortunately, I was deeply entangled in an affair with the spirit of poverty and didn't even know it. Like so many people, my pride blinded me to the depth of my bondage to this spirit.

I can remember being very critical of television ministers and people who preached "prosperity." The level of self-righteousness that I walked in was astounding. Despite my expertise on what the Bible says about finances, I found myself and my family falling deeper into the "poverty pit." At one point, I was so desperate to provide food for my family that I went to a plasma bank to give plasma for some Chinese food.

As I was sitting in the lobby of the plasma center, I looked around at the people who were there. I heard a voice speak very clearly, "What are you doing here?" As I pondered that question, the same voice spoke again, saying, "This is not your portion! Leave now!"

I immediately got up and walked out the door. I went to the car and told my wife that we were leaving. God provided food that night, but it left a lingering question: "If this is not my portion, then what is?" In my frustration, I asked God a question (or rather made a demand): "Teach me how to prosper!"

It was like a bell rang in my spirit. I knew immediately that there was a shift in the atmosphere. It was as if heaven was smiling on my question. I knew that God was saying, "Finally, you have asked the right question."

The first thing that God began to reveal to me is the law of seedtime and harvest or as I like to call it simply *the law of the seed.*

> *While the earth remaineth, seedtime and harvest, and cold and heat, and summer and winter, and day and night shall not cease* (Genesis 8:22 KJV).

Also during this time, I got hold of a book entitled *Supernatural Provision* by Joan Hunter. That book transformed my life. An impartation of prosperity came on me by reading the book and inculcating its teachings. Thank you, Momma Joan!

God began a process of training and instructing me on how to operate in the blessings of Abraham. The first assignment He gave me was to give. He told me to sow. In fact, God told me to give the last money I had. Because I am a man of great faith and power, you can imagine my reaction: "The devil is a liar!"

The moment I sowed, there was a shift in the atmosphere. Hours later, someone walked up to my wife and me and said that God had instructed him to give us the last money in his pocket. Hallelujah! I began to see firsthand the power of sowing. Not only did God reveal the supernatural law of seed time and harvest, but He taught me the power of gratitude.

I call this *the law of gratitude*. Victim mentality and gratitude cannot coexist within the same life. I had been very ungrateful. I murmured and complained all the time. No wonder it was so difficult for me to see breakthrough in my life and finances.

The more you complain in your trial, the longer you remain in your trial. This was a very difficult lesson for me to learn, but it has literally transformed my life.

Gratitude is a key to unlocking abundance in our lives. The more we are grateful, the more God graciously pours into our lives. When we complain, we are telling God that we cannot handle what He has given us.

As God continued to teach me this lesson and I continued to apply it to my life, the miracles and blessings became bigger and bigger. One day, after attending an event with my wife, a person walked up to us and handed us a check for over $20,000. I literally began to weep. I didn't realize it, but God had broken the back of the spirit of poverty in my life. It all began with the law of the seed and the law of gratitude. Keep sowing! Keep praising! Keep thanking God for His faithfulness, and things will turn around for you like they did for me.

Today, poverty and I are *not* on speaking terms. He doesn't like me and I don't like him, so we have agreed not to see or communicate with each other ever again. In fact, I have a restraining order on Mr. Poverty; he is not allowed within a 1,000-foot radius of where I am, and if he is already somewhere I am going, he must leave when I arrive.

The Law of Stewardship

Moreover, it is required of stewards that they be found faithful (1 Corinthians 4:2 ESV).

Stewardship is a very important principle that we must understand if we want to live in God's abundance. God will never consistently place resources in the hand of a poor steward. Waste and mismanagement are not part of God's vocabulary. Therefore, He will never allow His blessings to go to waste.

Think of this for a moment—condensation is absorbed from water and becomes rain. The rain falls from the sky to the earth and waters the ground. Plants and trees bud and bring forth fruit as a result; animals eat the fruit from the tree, and the cycle goes on. There is no waste! Any area of waste in our lives is an area that is not eligible for increase. As God taught me to be a better steward of what was in my hand, He was able to trust me with more.

Today, the cycle of poverty can be broken off your life once and for all. Pray this prayer with me:

Father, in the name of Jesus, I thank You that You are the God of all creation. You are the God of unlimited power and resources. I am Your child. I declare that Your abundance and increase flows in my life in the name of Jesus.

You are the God of more than enough; therefore, I have more than enough. Thank You for Your faithfulness. From this day forward, I will sow according to Your Word, and as You lead, I will maintain an attitude of gratitude. I will be a good steward of the resources You have entrusted to me in the name of Jesus. I declare that supernatural increase is my portion in Jesus' name. Amen!

Kynan Bridges

Kynan Bridges Ministries

info@kynanbridges.com

Chapter Eleven

OPPRESSION: HEALING THE MIND AND EMOTIONS OF THE OPPRESSED

When I was a young boy, I dealt with oppression, even though I didn't really recognize it as oppression. Most of our friends in the church where I grew up participated in sports, and the mindset was that to be a *real man*, you had to be a *sports* man. Sports were highly valued, and our church friends either bowled or played basketball, softball, or baseball. In fact, they participated in anything involving a ball!

But guess what? Ricky Renner was not gifted in *any* kind of sports involving a ball. I actually hated every kind of ball sport, and to this day I don't like any kind of sports that have to do with a ball. It always symbolized failure to me.

As a very young man, voices began to speak to me, saying, *There's something wrong with you. There's something really wrong. You can't compete with the other guys. You cannot do what the other guys can do.* Those thoughts kept striking my mind repeatedly.

When I went to school, I tried to be involved in sports with all the other guys. But still, I was such a failure when it came to sports. Every day, I would have those feelings of failure reinforced by voices speaking failure to me over and over and over again. This was an early assault on my mind, and because I didn't understand what was happening, I couldn't even verbalize it. I knew I was different from the other guys. I liked art, museums, and music, including the symphony. I liked creativity.

I was just wired differently. But the same voice that told me I was a failure for not being good at sports also repeatedly sneered, *You're a freak to like the things you like.* Those voices constantly lambasted me, day in and day out. I can still remember looking into the mirror as a young boy and thinking, *What is wrong with you? There's something really wrong with you.* It wasn't depression; it was an outside oppressive force trying to penetrate my mind and take me hostage.

When I was in the seventh grade, I became ill and missed half of the school year. During my absence, a new type of math had been introduced. When I finally returned to school, I had missed half a year of instruction, so I did not understand what was being taught. Not only was I struggling in math, but I also didn't do well in writing because I had missed so much about English grammar.

Every day I struggled. As I sat at my desk, I would hear voices speaking to my mind: *There's something wrong with you. You are inferior. You're a failure. You're stupid. You can't understand because you're stupid!* I constantly heard voices accusing me: *You're a failure because you are not athletic. You're a freak because you are so different from other people.*

Even though I had failed in mathematics, my teacher liked me and graduated me to the next level in school. That may seem like a good thing, but if I didn't understand math in the *seventh* grade, how was I going to understand math in the *eighth* grade? For another entire year, I struggled with mathematics as that relentless voice kept speaking to me: *There's something wrong with you. You're just stupid!* But that year, my eighth-grade teacher also liked me and passed me into the ninth grade.

When I entered ninth grade, we were going to study algebra. Well, my algebra teacher was so old that she had also been my *father's* algebra teacher! Unfortunately, when my father was a child, she did not like him. During my first day in class, as this teacher was taking roll, she came to my name and said, "Ricky Renner."

I responded, "Here."

She asked, "Is your father Ronald Renner?"

I answered, "Yes, that's my father."

I vividly remember her face as she pulled her glasses down to the end of her nose. She peered at me behind those thick lenses. Then she pushed her glasses back up onto her face and said matter-of-factly, "Stupid. In this class your name is *Stupid*. Any child of Ronald Renner is *stupid, stupid, stupid*—and that is your name in this class."

Notice what was happening. The devil was telling me I was a stupid failure and a freak. And now he was able to bring in reinforcements through this woman. He began to use someone who was an authority figure, with the power of influence, to reinforce the lies he had already been telling me.

Then when the other students heard what the teacher had called me, they thought it was hysterical. They all began to call me "Stupid." When I walked through the hallway at school, I would hear, "Hey Stupid! Hey Stupid, where are you going?"

Every day when that teacher called the roll in class, she would call everyone else by their actual name, but as soon as she came to my name, she would call out, "Stupid Renner."

And every time, I would compliantly answer, "Here."

If I raised my hand to ask a question, she would respond, "Yes, Stupid. Can somebody please help Stupid?"

I was labeled Stupid in that class and it spread to the hallways and the entire campus of that school.

The devil—*diabolos*—was striking and striking and striking to penetrate my mind so I would believe the lie that I was stupid, a failure, a freak, and that there was something very wrong with me. The devil was an outsider and a cruel dictator—an absolute tyrant trying to subdue, conquer, and dominate my young life. He was trying to convince me to believe the lie, because whatever we believe about ourselves becomes our reality. The devil knew if I began to believe what I was hearing, that lie would have eventually become my reality, and I would fail in life.

The devil wants us to believe his lies because if he can deceive us into believing a lie, that lie will become our reality. Oppression will leave the mental and spiritual realms, and it will become a reality in all areas of life.

Even though the devil was in pursuit of my destruction through his persistent lies, when I was fourteen years old, I gloriously received the baptism in the Holy Spirit, and those attacks ceased. When I received the baptism in the Holy Spirit, the power of God came on me and the devil's mission was aborted. All of those attacks stopped. He drove that darkness out of my life.

The devil is a tyrant and he wants to lord over people. He wants to tell us what to think, what to believe, and his goal is to feed us lie after lie trying to get us to take the bait and believe him. Then with that false mindset, we begin acting accordingly and our view of life and of ourselves changes radically for the worse.

That is what oppression is and how it operates.

Praise God, He makes a way of escape for all His children. Never give up. Never doubt your heavenly Father. He will show you the right path to follow.

Excerpt from *Healing the Mind and Emotions of the Oppressed* by Rick Renner

Rick Renner

www.renner.org

@RickRenner

Rick Renner is an author and highly respected Bible teacher. He has worked with the international Christian community for many years. He has written more than twenty books.

In 1991, Rick and his family moved to the Soviet Union. They have founded several churches in Russia—the Riga Good News Church in Latvia, the Moscow Good News Church, and the Kiev Good News Church in the capital of Ukraine.

Rick is the founder and director of the Good News Association of Pastors and Churches with nearly 800 member churches in Russia. He is also the founder of Media Mir, the first Christian television network that broadcasts the Gospel to an audience of 110 million people. Rick and his family reside in Moscow.

Chapter Twelve

MY ENCOUNTER WITH THE MASTER

When I was in elementary school, my friends and I began stealing wine from the local neighborhood store, which was directly across the street from the school. On my way to my first day in junior high, I was introduced to marijuana by a young man who had to repeat the ninth grade. (By the way, he is now deceased.)

In the ninth grade, I was introduced to cocaine, mescaline, and other amphetamines. By the time I was a young adult, I had experienced drugs, alcohol, cigarettes, fornication, lying, cheating, stealing, etc. Not to mention I had a foul mouth.

My mother made sure I became a Cub Scout, Boy Scout, and youth choir member. I also played a cornet, violin, and the bongos. I was always on the honor roll and was inducted into the National Honor Society. I went on to graduate from Western University for engineering.

Even though I grew up in a good home with a mother who *dragged* us to church, I would say that it reminds me of 2 Timothy 3:5: "Having a form of godliness but denying its power. And from such people turn away!" (NKJV). I had become a friend of the world and an enemy of God.

All that my mother tried to do didn't matter because when you are young, you are seeking your own identity. The devil wants a strong-willed, rebellious kid to recruit in his kingdom. Therefore, the devil and I partnered up so that he could *show* me the things that I thought were cool and exciting and not life-threatening. What a lie!

Throughout my adulthood, I was a chronic drug user. Many times, I was homeless or sleeping on someone's couch.

The devil is a good campaigner but a poor planner. I got mastered by his plan, but I then met the master planner, chief architect, and builder Jesus Christ.

You see, the devil said "Checkmate," but God said, "I don't think so!" God never runs out of moves.

The devil left me for dead, but God gave me *life!* He is a sovereign God with infinite wisdom who knows the end from the beginning.

With all the odds against me, I was hired by an automobile dealership on June 22, 2009. This dealership is about 15 miles from where my wife and I reside. I knew no one when I started there except the gentlemen who was instrumental in getting me hired. Actually, I had no choice because the "friend of the court" was on me like a cheap suit. Besides that, I was tired of being thrown in jail when I went to the court hearings.

Anyway, I worked while meditating on and quoting Scriptures because the only thing I had to stand on was the Word of God. I was no longer of the world. I witnessed so much injustice in the marketplace. While I waited on the Lord, others were getting deals from management and other staff.

Praise God, I had an account with Jesus. As time elapsed, He catapulted my sales like never before. I went on to become the number one new car sales professional. I have received different awards for the past eight years.

I had the opportunity to meet Joan Hunter during her conference in 2017 at the church we attend. She prayed for me and we have been friends since then. I now call her my big sister.

She had been a car sales professional several years ago, so we bonded. She has touched and agreed with me for an increase in my sales and it worked. *Praise God!*

> *May the Lord God of your fathers make you*
> *a thousand times more numerous than you*

are, and bless you as He has promised you!
(Deuteronomy 1:11 NKJV)

Today, my wife and I have a ministry for homeless pregnant adult women called H.I.S. Restoration Ministries in Saginaw, Michigan. My wife Lisa is the executive director.

God took someone who was counted out by the world and brought them into His fold. My life has never been the same.

We will continue to give Him all the praise, glory, and honor.

Lisa and I celebrated fifteen years of salvation and marriage in 2020.

I am so blessed!

Sammy Coleman

Sammy.coleman@labadieauto.com

Chapter Thirteen

TOO OLD? TOO SHORT? SURPRISE!

As women, wives, and mothers, we often sacrifice so much. Sometimes our dreams and hopes have to be put on hold in order to be present in the lives of our spouses, children, and family. For me, it was the dream of becoming a flight attendant.

We were on our first family vacation outside of Texas. We were excited because it would be the first time we would all fly together to our destination. There were only twenty passengers on the flight, and the nice flight attendant took time to sit and visit with us. She described her love for her job and I was intrigued by her story. The more she shared, the more I felt something stir within me.

She asked if I was bilingual because the airline industry was in desperate need of Spanish-speaking flight attendants. I told her I was bilingual and she highly encouraged me to apply. I was beyond thrilled and excited about the possibility, but reality would soon hit hard.

I realized I had a husband who needed me at home and children who needed me even more. I still had young children to raise who demanded everything from me. And I was too short in comparison to all the flight attendants I had ever seen. So there it went—my personal little dream was put on the shelf of "what ifs," never to be spoken or talked about.

But God!

Twenty-one years later while working for Joan Hunter Ministries, my personal dream would resurface. I had the great honor and blessing of being part of the traveling team for the ministry. During one of my flights, the Lord brought me full circle to my dream.

I happened to be flying alone that day and the flight attendant made an announcement over the PA system. They needed a Spanish-speaking person to translate for a passenger who needed help. I immediately walked to the front and assisted the passenger.

As I made my way back to my seat, I felt like the flood gates of heaven opened. I had a glimpse of my dream. I was having a God-given thought: "I could be that flight attendant now." I struggled with that thought because I really enjoyed my job at Joan Hunter Ministries. The Lord had gifted me with my present position, so why would He move me out of it now? I also loved living life with my coworkers, who were more like family.

Could it be that the Lord was now moving me to serve His children in the workplace? Whatever it was, I just couldn't shake it off. After much prayer and discussion with my husband, I eventually mustered up the courage to research the airline's webpage for the requirements to become a flight attendant. It was very evident this would not be an easy process because it's a very competitive career. It takes years to secure such a position with the airlines, not to mention the required four-week rigorous training which would take me away from home. Many applicants fail to successfully pass this training.

As a fifty-three-year-old woman, I was finally an empty-nester. We had raised our children and encouraged them to chase their dreams. I decided it was time to put myself on the list and pursue my own dream. I thought, "If not now, when?"

When I contemplated which airline I wanted to work for, I soon knew there was only one well-loved airline to consider. I researched their website and was immediately disappointed to learn that the window of accepting applications had closed. The next opportunity wouldn't open for several years. I soon discovered that out of the 28,000-plus applications received during their forty-eight-hour window, the airline only planned on hiring 2 to 5 percent.

At my age, the odds were against me. I felt I was too old and too short to be accepted. I saw my flight attendant dream slowly fading away, but I trusted the Lord because in the end He was the one who was directing my path toward my God-given destiny. I just released it all to Him and put it in His hands.

Ultimately, I trusted His perfect will in my life. Deep inside, I felt it was also okay to ask Him for the impossible because He is my Abba Father, and what child doesn't ask their father for something he/she desperately desires?

It was also during this time that Joan Hunter gave a prophetic word about the Lord fulfilling long-lost dreams. I felt that word resonate within my spirit. I grabbed it and received it for myself. I presented my request to the Lord and continued on with my life.

Within twenty-four hours of my prayer, I happened to see an announcement from my desired airline: "bilingual flight attendants needed." They would only be accepting applications for the next forty-eight hours.

I couldn't believe this! Could this really be happening? Could I really pass all the required bilingual tests? Would I advance to the phone interview? Would I be invited to a face-to-face interview at their headquarters? Would I be offered the coveted CJO (contingency job offer)? Could I really step away from my life as I had known it, my husband, my children, and my grandchildren to take part in the required four-week intensive training? Would I pass this test and get hired?

In the end, the Lord made a way where there seem to be no way, and the doors opened wide. Through His ability working through me and His unfailing favor, I successfully became a bilingual flight attendant at the age of fifty-three, working for one of the top sought-after airlines. Something I could have never imagined for myself, but I knew that if it was meant to be, nothing on earth could come between me and my delayed dream.

The definition of *delay* is "postpone or defer," but it doesn't mean "never." As I began my second act, my next career move, I knew that everything

I had experienced thus far had prepared me for this season in my life. What a beautiful adventure the Lord set before me that has allowed me the opportunity to serve thousands of people and many in their native language. All along it was in His perfect timing. What a peaceful place to be.

Sara Alaniz

sararalaniz@gmail.com

Chapter Fourteen

GIVE GOD THE GLORY

Steve Harvey has a powerful testimony of not quitting and has often shared his remarkable story. He was raised in a single-parent household. At a young age, he became homeless, lived in a car, and had $35 to his name.

He cried out to God and begged Him for help. He sensed in his heart that if he got up and tried, everything would work out for his good. He didn't understand how, he just knew something was about to happen.

He certainly could have quit! But instead, he pushed through!

Steve called his voicemail and there was a message from Chuck Suttonwith from *Showtime at the Apollo* in New York City, asking him to come to the Apollo on Sunday night. They really liked his material and they wanted to put him on TV.

Steve was in Pensacola, Florida and only had $35. Certainly, that was not enough to get him to New York City. He thought, "Maybe they want me for next Sunday." That would give him some time to make the money he needed to travel to New York City.

His dream was to be on TV some day in the future. He really felt God was giving him this opportunity. Steve listened to the message again and again to verify the date he was to be there.

He found a second message on his voicemail that hadn't been there when he heard the first message. The second message was an invitation to do a comedy act in Jacksonville, Florida only three and a half hours away from where he was! Steve confirmed the request and was told he'd make $150 if he was able to make it for the Friday night gig. He got the message on Thursday and headed for Jacksonville.

The owner of the club liked his routine so much that he asked him to stay the next night as well. Steve made $300 in two nights of stand-up comedy.

Steve now had the airfare needed to go to New York City! God had provided and he was so thankful. Steve flew to New York City and was able to appear that Sunday night on *Showtime at the Apollo*.

He performed at the Apollo. His show was televised. Steve was on TV. His dream had been satisfied. They liked him so much, they hired him back.

Steve had a dream. He asked God for help to realize that dream. God was faithful. Today, Steve is on TV daily and has had several programs of his own. He no longer is just a guest; he is the star of the show.

Steve still gives God the glory for picking him up off the street and giving him the opportunity to shine his light for Jesus.

Chapter Fifteen

MY JOURNEY TO DANCE

When I was five years old, my mother and father came to us, their five children, and announced they had a big surprise for us. They had been saving money so each of us children could take lessons. We could choose either piano lessons or dance lessons; however, we couldn't do both.

Being the youngest, I got to choose last. My immediate response was, "I want to take both!" My parents lovingly explained that there wasn't enough money for both. I chose piano and it turned out to be a wonderful part of my life along with playing the flute. In my heart, however, I always longed to dance.

Once I got married and had children, there always seemed to be something else we needed to spend our money on. Dancing got pushed to the very back burner.

One morning a few years ago, I woke up and thought, "This is it! If I don't learn to dance now, I never will!"

Another unusual thing began to happen around this time. I noticed that every time I went to a conference of some kind, if there was any kind of music at all, especially praise music, all I wanted to do is to jump up and dance! With no training at all, I was a little self-conscious, but my heart would not let me stay seated!

One time in Chicago, I was in a faith-based conference. A man I had never met walked up to me and told me that he had a word for me. He said he had seen me walk past and had inquired of the Lord about me. He told me that the Lord had responded, "This lady lives to praise Me!"

Wow! I had never heard such a thing before. So I got to thinking about the idea of dance as a way to praise the Lord.

My dream had always been to learn how to do the waltz. I love watching people waltz across the floor. When I was little, I had even tried to waltz on ice skates.

Finally, I got up the courage and signed up for ballroom dance classes. I loved it! One day, my phone rang. The lady on the other end said she was from an organization that was hosting a huge gala to help raise money for underprivileged children who wanted music lessons. They were hosting a Dancing with the Stars competition in a few months and asked if I would consider being a celebrity dancer in the competition! I almost fell out of my chair!

After months and months of practice, aching feet, and avoiding hurricanes, the competition finally took place one Saturday night. I was the oldest dancer there! To my absolute joy and surprise, my professional dance coach Allan Alday and I won the championship first place trophy!

It was one of the most exciting experiences in my life!

Teri Secrest

www.TeriSecrest.com

Join me on Facebook

Watch me on YouTube

A Word from Joan

Teri Secrest is an excellent example of pursuing a dream at any cost! As a child, she always wanted to learn how to play the piano and how to dance. She couldn't take dance lessons until later in life; however, she did become an accomplished pianist playing a wide variety of genres ranging from contemporary to classical. Her first love was always to worship God.

Later in life, after the age of 50, she wanted to fulfill her dream of dancing. Teri wanted to be able to worship the Lord with graceful dancing like she'd never experienced before. She is very tall and wanted to learn how to dance with great grace and skill.

When the worship team was playing during meetings, she would flow with the music and dance with such a high level of grace and ease, despite her unusual dance build. Teri became absolutely breathtaking to watch and landed herself a position on a fundraiser for disadvantaged children. She and her dancing partner were awarded a score of 10 out of 10 from all the judges!

What dreams are lying dormant in your heart? Follow Teri's example and you might be surprised where God takes you! His thoughts are higher than our thoughts, and His ways are higher than our ways.

Chapter Sixteen

INVEST IN THE PROMISE

We moved our family from southeast Georgia to north Texas during Thanksgiving break in November 2006. It was both a great adventure and an upheaval for our family. One of our daughters, Emily, was in the fifth grade when we arrived here to carve out a new life together. It was a bumpy ride, and we did the best we could to navigate all the changes this brought to our family.

I have always believed that our children come pre-wired from heaven with all the seeds of their destiny contained within them. To that end, we do our best to pay attention to their gifts, personalities, and natural strengths so we can support in them what we discern God has created them to be. Emily is disciplined, creative, musical, and intelligent. She prefers to be with a few close friends than with a large party of people, she will work diligently to bring something to perfection, and she has a quick and clever wit.

At the beginning of sixth grade, she wanted to try out for band. Because she was in her school's gifted and talented program, the band directors liked to encourage the harder instruments (like French horn, oboe, and bassoon) to that group of students. From the moment Emily put the mouthpiece of the French horn to her lips, she knew that was the instrument for her. She was able to make music on the first try—not an easy task.

Thus, our journey with the Texas band program began. By Christmas, Emily had advanced to the eighth-grade honors band and was playing well beyond where a beginner should be. We were encouraged to seek out a private lesson teacher for her.

That sounds great, except...

Well, we had risked everything to make the leap to Texas and start our own business. It took all our resources to get here; our finances were stretched as tightly as they could be. The business was just beginning to take off when the rug was pulled out from under us. Our largest client declared bankruptcy, and we had been left holding the bag. Then as the housing bubble burst, one by one we had nine clients declare bankruptcy, and the bulk of our other clients tapered off their business with us to survive. We went from tight to under water in a flash.

But here was this child, given to us by God to nurture, develop, protect, and steward. She clearly had a gift from God, and by placing us in Keller, Texas, we lived five miles from one of the premier private lesson studios in the region. That could not have been by accident. I was not willing to go into debt for lessons, so I began to pray about it.

I swallowed my pride, went to visit with her band directors (who, by the way, were totally awesome), and asked them for their advice. They all recognized a gift in her as well as her fierce dedication to learn the fundamentals, practice, and play. They offered a half scholarship for private lessons for her through their band booster program. Gratefully, we accepted and decided we would find a way to invest in her gift, whatever sacrifice that required.

One afternoon, we got a call from the school nurse. "Whatever it is you are doing right now, I think you need to drop and come directly to the school as soon as possible. Emily has broken her arm."

Well, a broken arm is no fun, but the urgency in her voice unnerved us. We jumped in the car and went straight there. The moment I saw Emily, I understood the urgency. Her little arm was curved like an "S." She was in shock, and so were we.

Being self-employed, we were without good health insurance. Panic began to rise in me as the doctor read her x-rays and told us she needed surgery and would have to have plates and screws in both the bones in her forearm, followed by extensive physical therapy to regain full use of her arm.

So not only was there no extra money for private lessons, we now had nearly $10,000 of medical debt on top of us. We felt buried under it all and considered dropping private lessons as they seemed like a luxury. Besides, Emily had suffered a huge setback. The broken arm was the one she used to finger the horn's keys, and it would be months before she was well enough to resume playing.

Most kids would have lost interest. Most kids wouldn't practice if they had a tiny cut on their finger. Not Emily. She had us prop her French horn on one pillow, with another wedged to hold it against her knees so she could blow into the mouthpiece as she stretched her good arm across the horn to finger (backward) and continue practicing.

Clearly, there was something to this child's determination. Emily's private instructor had recommended she audition for the Greater Dallas

Youth Orchestra (GDYO), and auditions were scheduled the weekend she broke her arm. Was that a sign or an obstacle?

The Fort Worth Junior Symphony Orchestra held their auditions much later than GDYO, so Emily set herself a goal to be prepared—injury and all—and try out for a spot. She made the orchestra! And now, on top of money for lessons, we had fees for the orchestra and a weekly three-hour rehearsal and concerts to drive her to in downtown Fort Worth. More sacrifice. More expense. More glimpses of God's gift awakening in our child.

The season with FWJSO ended, and when auditions came around again, she set her sights on GDYO (a more prestigious organization). She easily made the orchestra and was often their principal horn. On top of marching band fees and commitments, concert band, and private lessons, we now added a five-hour rehearsal each Sunday evening in downtown Dallas at the Sammons Center for the Arts. All of this was quite an investment of time and money.

The Texas Music Educators Association (TMEA) holds annual competitions for each district, region, and area, and finally, all-state. It is a highly competitive program, and at the time Emily was involved, more than 50,000 students participated in the process with only about one percent of them making it as far as all-state. Typically, only juniors and seniors advanced to the state level. However, Emily made all-state all four years of high school and landed as the top French horn player in the state of Texas two of those four years.

She also continued playing with GDYO, and a tour through Europe was an amazing opportunity for her to travel with fellow musicians, interact with new cultures, and gain valuable experience. The price tag was well beyond our reach. Emily was crestfallen, and so were we. As the date for the first deposit drew near, we knew we just could not swing it.

When Emily did not turn in paperwork to go, the orchestra's program director called us. With a heavy heart, I had to tell him Emily would not be able to join them on tour because we just did not have the funds available to make the trip. He paused for a moment and said the maestro was really counting on Emily for the tour. In fact, he had chosen a specific piece of music with a significant horn solo in it for Emily to play. He instantly offered us a half scholarship, wanting Emily to have the opportunity.

That night, we held a family meeting. A half scholarship was amazing! An answer to prayer, but the remaining half was still going to be a hardship. I had tears in my eyes as our other daughter, Kate, volunteered that if we didn't go on any sort of family vacation that year, we could use the money to send Emily to Europe. In fact, I still tear up at this, knowing how much Kate loves to travel. It was a true sacrifice from her heart to support her sister's opportunity, and I was totally undone by it.

That is, in fact, what we decided to do. We came up with the money, and off to Europe Emily went to gain the experience and deepen her connection to the orchestra's personnel. In the fall, she began her senior year of high school, and we began to turn our attention to college music programs and the audition process for that. Emily was now in her second year as drum major with all those responsibilities, still participating in band competitions, the TMEA process, her final season with GDYO, maintaining her grades, and now narrowing down which schools we would travel to for in-person auditions for college.

The whole year is a blur. It seemed as if all I did was drive places, fill out forms, and write checks. The audition process for colleges is crazy, with much riding on those appointments. In the end, she narrowed her choices down to two; it would either be Baylor University or Texas Christian University. Both are great schools with great music programs, but as private universities, a pretty high price tag to go with that.

In the meantime, it was her last TMEA all-state competition. Once again, she made state and landed as the number one French horn in Texas. She got to have her pick of the ensembles, a formality. They call your name, and you choose your ensemble. Of course, the top horn will choose to play as principal in the top orchestra ensemble. Except Emily did not do that.

When they called her name, she did not choose the Symphony Orchestra. She skipped down eight spots to play as the principal horn for the 5A Symphonic Band. This was unheard of! Who would give up the top spot in the top ensemble?

At this point, it was the love of music, not the competition that motivated her. As it turns out, that band was going to be conducted by Dr. Frank Ticheli, and they were going to play one of his pieces, "Angels in the Architecture," which was one of Emily's favorite band/chorale pieces. She could not pass up the opportunity to work with the composer and play the piece with him as the conductor, so she chose to participate in his ensemble.

That got everyone's attention. Across the next few days, Emily worked hard and had a few opportunities to visit with Dr. Ticheli, who would forever remember that she gave up the top orchestra to play his piece with him.

Okay, now we can fast forward to decision time for college. Both Baylor and TCU offered Emily some significant scholarship money to attend their schools. However, Baylor was definitely in the lead with their offer. We liked many things about both schools, but because Emily was so well known in the DFW area and because TCU was close to home, I was leaning in that direction.

Still, from both schools there was going to be a tuition gap that needed to be filled, regardless. We did play one school against the other, and both offers came up but had not made it to the status of "full ride" for which we had hoped.

Along the way, Emily communicated with the brass faculty at TCU that she appreciated their offer, but it looked like she would accept Baylor's offer. It just so happened that TCU had commissioned work from Dr. Ticheli, and he was there with the brass faculty as they discussed incoming freshman and scholarship offers. Emily's name came up.

Dr. Ticheli's ears perked up. He remembered the curly-blonde French horn who gave up eight spots and the top ensemble to come play his piece at TMEA. He strongly encouraged the TCU faculty to do what they needed to do not to let Emily get away. She would be an asset to their program.

At the eleventh hour, an offer for a full-ride scholarship was extended. Not only that, but it was extended for all four years of her education, and should a fifth year be needed to complete the program, the scholarship would remain available through year five. Tuition at the time was $58,000 per year! Emily became a TCU Horned Frog and joined the Horn Frog Band!

Her time with the GDYO was finished. She had aged out of the orchestra and was in her first year of college. One afternoon, Emily received a call from the program director. The orchestra was preparing to tour China over the summer, and the maestro would like for her to join the tour and play for the orchestra once more. Once again, he offered her a half scholarship. Emily told him how excited she was about the prospect and let him know she would need to discuss it with her parents before she could accept.

I was on a ministry trip, so she could not reach me until late that evening. This time, we had the money available to send her, even without the scholarship. We had come a long, long way. "Of course, you should go!" I told her. "Call Chuck tomorrow and tell him the news!"

The next morning, before she had a chance to call the GDYO office, her phone rang. "Emily, we have talked it over, and we would like to cover the expenses for your entire trip—including the cost of your travel visa! Would that help you make up your mind?"

Off to China she went.

When she returned, she entered her sophomore year of college and continued her incredible experience with the TCU Horn Studio, Symphony Orchestra, and various ensembles as well as playing multiple professional gigs. She maintained a horn studio where she taught more than 70 students individual private lessons, and she graduated Magna Cum Laude with a Bachelor's in Horn Performance. At the time of this testimony, she is about to enter her second year of the Master's program at Eastman School of Music in Rochester, New York—also with a significant scholarship and stipend.

Why am I sharing this with you? I want to encourage you to pay attention to what God has given you in terms of preferences, personality, gifts, and abilities. Pay attention to this in your children. Invest in stewarding these gifts to the best of your ability. Stretch yourself to develop your skills, leverage your opportunities, and, in so doing, honor what God has created you to be.

Consider King David when he replied to King Araunah, "No, but I will buy it from you for a price. I will not offer burnt offerings to the Lord my God that cost me nothing" (2 Sam. 24:24 ESV). What we present to the Lord *should cost us something*. It shouldn't be a cakewalk or handed to us without effort. What we bring to God should involve investment, sacrifice, discipline, and drive. That's what stewardship requires.

Sometimes, it might not seem practical to invest in education or travel, coaching or mentoring (or private lessons). I can assure you, the return on your investment will be rewarded. First identify, then cooperate with the gifts God has given you. Invest in them, and watch the miraculous favor that follows.

Wendy K Walters

wendykwalters.com

A Word from Joan

Wendy wears numerous hats. Among them are writer, mentor, ghostwriter, author, editor, personal adviser, executive coach, and branding expert. She is an exciting, entertaining inspirational speaker to every audience. She has guided numerous authors from an idea to a manuscript to a published book.

Wendy is an amazing, anointed, gifted woman of God. She is filled with the wisdom and Word of God and equipped with experience and influence in the marketplace. When Wendy Walters speaks, activation follows. She combines the practical with the prophetic and big things happen!

Chapter Seventeen

JESUS

The ultimate example of a person who never quit in the face of opposition is our Lord and Savior, Jesus Christ. We so often think and talk about His travels, His love and kindness to all He met and ministered to. For a few minutes, think of all He faced:

God sent Him to a damaged and challenging existence on earth. Jesus had to leave the throne and peace of Heaven to be born as a helpless child. He had to learn how to walk, talk, and exist on this planet. He felt pain and bled just like we do. When He reached His time for ministry, He was enticed and tempted by the devil himself. While out in a desert without food and water, Jesus fought His enemy and got the victory.

Jesus experienced the love of parents and family, but also endured the pain of rejection, slander, and eventual execution on the cruel cross. He was loved by many; however, His earthly enemies falsely accused Him, tortured Him, and crucified Him. Yes, behind it all was satan who wanted to destroy the blessed Son of God.

We know the story, but do you look at the negative portions of His life as well as the positive love, joy, and peace His pictures so often portray?

Life brings challenges and frustrations whether you are the Son of God or an adopted child of God. Jesus knew before His miraculous birth that He would die on that cross for the sins of the world. That means He died for you and for me before we were even thought of or born. God designed the plan for our salvation, for our destiny.

Yes, we endure some late nights of pain and tears; but in the end, God uses our pain, our tears, and our love to bring us to the exact destiny He designed so long ago. We all would like to stay in peace and joy with constant happiness. However, our spiritual growth is formed by the challenges we survive and subsequently share with others as a testimony of God's goodness, grace, and mercy.

We are instructed to act like God and shape our lives more like Jesus. We are to be the hands, feet, voice, and love of Jesus working through us. To understand and embrace His love, we must focus on the prize, not the agony of the path to get there. Jesus kept His eyes and focus on the other side of the Cross—on His resurrection and the salvation of God's children. He knew what the prize was and He also knew the price He would have to pay.

Jesus didn't falter. Jesus didn't quit! He fulfilled His destiny! He faced His accusers and spoke only the words that came from His Father in Heaven!

When you face your next challenge, think of what He had to do to give you the opportunity to live with Him forever. He had a God-ordained destiny, you have one too.

Don't quit! Jesus never gave up on you! Don't you ever even think of giving up on Him!

Instead, reach out for His outstretched hand. Jesus is always there waiting for your prayer. Ask for His help every day. His Holy Spirit is waiting for your request so He can work all things out for your good.

Never, *never, never quit!*

Chapter Eighteen

FAITH IT UNTIL YOU MAKE IT

Many prophecies have guided my life. I am stubbornly following God's leading. My goal is to stay on the path leading to my God-ordained destiny.

In approximately 2010, Joan Hunter came to our church in Shelby, North Carolina to minister. I saw amazing miracles that night. At that moment, I knew there was a God-ordained connection. I knew God had sent her to our church to change the direction of my life forever.

She had no idea I was just eighteen years of age when she gave me a prophetic word that night. She said God had called me to the NFL and He would use me in a mighty way.

As I was playing football in high school, I had hurt my ankle and had a concussion. I had to quit playing. I tried out for the football team at college. I was accepted and played football again. Unfortunately, I damaged my hamstring.

This was very frustrating for me. I knew I had the call of God on my life. God had a special plan for me but both legs had been damaged.

Eventually, God did heal me. In the interim, I could have gotten very discouraged, given up, gained weight, sat around the house, and allowed my muscles to turn to fat.

My other choice was to pursue the call of God on my life. I chose God and continued to work out. I exercised daily, ran daily, and practiced football moves daily. I was getting better and better and better. I kept my body in optimal condition.

I knew 2020–2021 would be the season when I would get picked up by an NFL team.

I knew that God would make a way for me to play football again. Any time I would get discouraged, I would call Ms. Joan for prayer. She would pray for me and give me clarity in my vision. I continued to prepare for my future.

In the process, I tried out for an NFL team and did very well at the tryouts. For some reason, they didn't hire me.

I could so easily have given up. I had done everything I knew to do to be the best I could be. Would I continue to pursue the word of the Lord or go another direction? I chose to continue to condition my body so I would be prepared to accept that opportunity when it came along.

My parents had moved to Hawaii. I joined them. I continued to work out and keep my body in good fighting condition.

I could have started questioning God. There were no prospects within sight. I called Ms. Joan again.

Joan gave me another word: "Timing is everything."

I believe I am very close to being chosen by an NFL team. I have chosen not to quit. I want to play football.

God spoke to me so many times. I know He has a great plan for my life. I choose to believe Him and His Word. I believe the words spoken by His prophets. I will not give up—never, never, never.

As I write this testimony, I am continuing my training. I am determined to reach the dream God first gave me years ago.

I am totally convinced that *"Miracles Happen!"*

Michael Gullatte

Michaelrgullatte@gmail.com

A Word from Joan

Many times, Michael would get discouraged and would hurt here or hurt there. I would call to pray for him and encourage him along the way. He would get healed and go on.

I have saved Michael's testimony for the last because many of you are right where Michael is at the moment. You are waiting while you are hanging on to your dream.

Did you hear God? Yes, you did! I want to encourage you to hang on and pursue your dream until you reach your God-given destiny and all He has in store for you. Whatever your goal is, continue to strive toward it. Don't give up. Never, never, never quit!

What dreams have you put on hold? Were these dreams from God or just on a wish list? If they were truly from God, list them:

_____

_____

_____

_____

_____

Start your research now. What do you have to do to prepare to reach your goal?

_____

_____

_____

_____

_____

Who is available and willing to encourage you and pray for you as you go forward?

_____

_____

_____

_____

_____

ABOUT JOAN HUNTER

Her focus is to train and equip believers to take the healing power of God beyond the four walls of the church and into the four corners of the earth! Joan's genuine approach and candid delivery enables her to connect intimately with people from all walks of life. Some describe her as being like Carol Burnett with the anointing of Jesus.

Joan ministers the Gospel with manifestations of supernatural signs and wonders in healing school sessions, miracle services, conferences, and churches around the world. Being sensitive to the Holy Spirit, Joan speaks prophetically in the services, releasing personal and corporate prophetic ministry to those in attendance.

At the young age of 12, Joan dedicated her heart to the Lord and has faithfully served him from that day to this. She has uncompromising faith and dedication to the call of God on her life. She exhibits a sincere desire to see the body of Christ set free in their body, mind, soul, spirit and finances.

Joan Hunter is a compassionate minister, dynamic teacher, an accomplished author, and an anointed healing evangelist.

Joan has ministered in countries all over the world and has been on numerous television and radio appearances. She has been featured on Sid Roth's *It's Supernatural, My New Day, Everlasting Love* with Patricia King and on *Today with Marilyn* (Hickey) *and Sarah*. Joan hosts a powerful and exciting show of her own called *Miracles Happen!*.

She has authored more than 18 books and has recorded teachings that will encourage you and teach you how to pray for the sick and them recover. Books and teachings are available to order through joanhunter.org. Some resources are available as digital downloads through Amazon.com and iTunes.

Joan Hunter and her husband, Kelley, live northwest of Houston, TX. Together, they have 4 daughters, 4 sons, 3 sons-in-law and 7 grandchildren. Joan is the daughter of the Happy Hunters, Charles & Frances Hunter.